THE SOWER

My Journey of Proclaiming God's Threefold Mercy

A Memoir By Michael 'Mo' Jones

"Sow for yourselves righteousness; reap steadfast love; break up your fallow ground, for it is the time to seek the Lord, that he may come and rain righteousness upon you."
Hosea 10:12 ESV

The sower sows the Word (Mark 4:14) to all different types of soil. It is not the sower's concern whether the seed will take root and grow, but rather being obedient to sowing the good news of Christ Crucified.

Father, please give us opportunities to sow Your Word into the hearts of those around us. Amen!

CHAPTER 1
"New Creation"

"Therefore, if anyone is in Christ, he is a new creation. The old has passed away; behold, the new has come." 2 Corinthians 5:17 ESV

The Next Day

There was something different inside me the next morning when I woke up. I felt as though my old way of life, my old way of thinking, was done with. I had an expectation that there was something new on the horizon. I didn't know what to think and was having a hard time processing all of this. I thought maybe what happened at the pool hall last night was a dream of some kind or maybe my mind was playing tricks on me. It just didn't make sense, yet I still had a peace inside me.

As I laid there in bed all morning, I reasoned that I am going to have to tell others what happened. Everyone around me knew that I dropped out of college because of the carpal tunnel. I was wearing braces on my wrists and needing surgery according to the doctors. But when they see me playing my bass with no issues, I'm going to have to say something as to why my hands are not numb and in pain. They are going to wonder what's going on.

I started going through my head how to tell others that I'm a follower of Christ Jesus and my carpel tunnel is now healed. I thought to myself maybe I should change my voice as I share this Good News with others. You know, like a superhero voice. Or maybe lift my hand in the air and say it as someone who is in a room to make an announcement. This thought made me laugh. I have always been one to make light of something before I would get serious about it. Laughter is always good for the soul. As I struggled believing that I was saved and healed I thought to myself "What if I tell someone I'm healed and then the carpal tunnel comes back and makes me look like a fool. I don't want to look like a fool." Yes, I had doubts- you could say. It's not every day you hear about someone you personally know being miraculously healed of a physical challenge or disease.

I remember looking at my hands and being so thankful that the numbness and pain were gone. I felt as though this restoration back to God Almighty was a new beginning. It was like my hands were now meant for doing something bigger than myself. How could I doubt what the Lord Jesus did for me? I just kept staring at my hands in amazement because it was hard to believe that I didn't have carpal tunnel anymore. I would clench my fists to reassure me that my strength was reclaimed. This would continue to build confidence that I was actually healed for His Glory.

The Holy Spirit was very patient with me and even though I doubted. He would continue to encourage and remind me that I really was forgiven and healed. That I was actually restored back to the Father through the ministry of reconciliation. He kept putting in my spirit that this testimony was going to help others see that Christ Jesus is real. I had this feeling that I am now a soldier of Christ and had an obligation to make Him known by proclaiming Christ Crucified. Telling others that He is alive, and He wants to restore His people back to Him.

Go And Tell

The Holy Spirit was making it obvious to go and tell people **what** happened to me and **how** it happened to me. He said, "Do not apologize to anyone for being bold even though fear will be right there to try and stop you from telling others." This was important for Him to tell me this, because I had already reasoned that in telling others it would create too much conflict. I thought no one would believe me and they would make fun of me, just like the first time I shared Christ when I was a young boy.

Conflict was always an issue with me. I avoided it as much as possible, because I could never think of a proper response of what to say while in the moment of conflict. Then, after the conflicting interaction, I would think about what I should've said while in that moment. I just wasn't quick with words and how to react when confronted. This would always create fear and insecurity within me and make me feel inferior and stupid.

I was intimidated by the idea to go and tell others. I wondered why I had to tell anybody about what happened. Then I thought how could I *not* tell anyone what happened? People need to know what the Lord had done- that Christ Jesus saved me and healed me of my sin and carpal tunnel! Besides, everyone knows about my carpal tunnel and how it affected my bass playing. People will wonder how I'm able to play the bass without struggling. I had to have an answer as to how my carpel tunnel is gone. Deep down, I just felt that when I tell others the good news of what Christ Jesus did for me, it would create conflict. But the Holy Spirit was working with me to push through this fear of conflict.

Boldness

Of course, there has to be resistance to telling others the Good News of Christ like a battle of good and evil. With one side trying to persuade me to keep my mouth shut through creating a fear of rejection, and the other side simply encouraging me to tell others. The one voice inside me would create conflict by telling me "No one will listen to you Mike - you will just look like a fool." The voice would also tell me that "No one wants to hear about Christ Jesus. He's just a hoax Mike, so don't make yourself look stupid." This was hard for me because I didn't want to make myself look stupid, that's for sure. On the other hand, I really wanted to tell others what happened.

Then there was that quiet calm voice of the Holy Spirit reminding me, through encouragement, of what He already told me: I was to tell others **what** happened and **how** it happened to me. He encourages me to speak with boldness and be not afraid. What was in the past is in the past. This is a new beginning. Then He kept reminding me that God forgave me of my sin and healed my carpal tunnel, and He wanted me to say it out of my mouth to tell others. The other voices inside me would say "don't say it," like they were mad. The Holy Spirit bearing witness with my spirit strongly encouraged me to speak it out of my mouth "I will be bold and be not afraid," and "God forgave me of my sin, and He healed my carpal tunnel." I started to speak this out of my mouth. The other voices continued to try and convince me to shut my mouth, but I just kept saying what the Holy Spirit told me to say louder and louder. It was building up within me the courage to believe what the Holy Spirit was putting in my spirit, and because of that, the other voices eventually stopped.

As I continued saying this out loud to build up my confidence, I became convinced that I was forgiven and healed. Done deal. I now believe. I then realized that **being bold is not how loud you can say something, but rather how convinced that what you are saying is true.** I realized that what is in my heart, or spirit, is what I will believe. Jesus said, *"Out of the abundance of the heart, the mouth speaks,"* (Matthew 12:34 ESV). This kind of boldness was something I always wanted even as an unbeliever, so I was excited that the Holy Spirit was teaching me how to be bold. This would end up being a huge first step for me, as I started this journey of now being indwelled with the Holy Spirit. I had a feeling that things would not be the same anymore.

I Start To Tell Others

I figured that I should first start with telling my family

what God Almighty has done for me. I went out of my bedroom and told my parents first. They seemed to receive what God put on my heart to say. They were a little hesitant at first, but I cannot blame them for that. They knew this carpal tunnel was sending me into episodes of depression and ruining my life. Maybe they thought I was fabricating the story to ease the depression. I just remember them cautiously agreeing with me as they nodded their heads as I told them that I was saved and healed. After I was done telling them, they gave me hugs and were happy for me.

My group of friends invited me to a get-together they were having that weekend. I thought this would be a perfect time to share with them the good news of what God has done for me. As I was driving to pick up my girlfriend Regine, I would rehearse scenarios out loud in my car. I knew that some of them would be skeptical, and I wanted to be ready on how to respond to their skepticism. When Regine got in the car, I told her I was going to share what God Almighty has done at this gathering we were going to. She thought this was a great idea.

When we got there, the first person I told was my best friend Micah. At first, he was a little shocked to hear the news. He was in the trenches since the beginning of this carpal tunnel. He did the typical Micah scratch the side of his head to think about what he just heard. I stood there smiling waiting for him to process what I was saying. He was amazed at what I told him and asked me to shake his hand. This was a test to prove that I had strength in my hands. Needless to say, when our hands connected, he could tell that what I was saying to him was true, because I had my strength back in my hands. It was a way for us to connect as best friends. He was excited with me about this change in my life.

As I was sharing this Good News of what the Lord has done in my life I came across the skeptics of this group of friends. There were two of them. After I was done telling them what God Almighty had done, they told me that it was all in my head and my carpal tunnel was not healed by God. They tried explaining to me that the mind has the ability to heal the body or even trick your body into thinking it's healed. The Holy Spirit quickly reminded me to be bold and not back down and not allow this skeptical claim to sway my thinking. I did what the Holy Spirit told me to do, and I boldly stood my ground.

I said "There is no other way I could have been healed. It was God Almighty who healed me, not my mind."

Then I continued "He healed my mind, spirit, body and soul and it was God and Him only who could do that."

They knew my story of dropping out of college because the carpal tunnel was so bad. Seeing me able to play bass again made it undeniable that I was healed. They did not want to give God the glory for it and wanted me to say it was my mind that healed me. I don't think so!! Jesus gets the credit and the glory! I didn't back down and spoke boldly of what the Lord had done. When they laughed at me and scoffed at me, I was surprised that it didn't bother me.

My other friends at this gathering embraced the idea that it was God who healed me of the carpal tunnel. I really didn't know if they were saved or not, but I was happy they received my testimony. I have to say it was a huge relief to only have a little confrontation. But this was a big step for me because I was so nervous and anxious as to how others would react. I had to start telling others my testimony, and my family and sphere of friends was a great place to start.

Cussing

One of the noticeable changes that happened right away was I could not cuss anymore or say anything vulgar and crude. This was a common practice of the tongue for me when around friends. When I was out shooting pool or bowling, my mouth would not have a filter. It just seemed normal for me to let my mouth get out of control. It was a peer pressure thing where certain people would bring that kind of junk out of my mouth. It wasn't their fault that I cussed. I just wanted to fit in. I didn't cuss or say anything crude when I was with my family. It was when I was in a certain place with certain people that I would let my tongue loose.

There was a guy I used to work with at Colonial Lanes who cussed and said vulgar things just as much or even more than me. While working with him he had a habit of saying "Jesus Christ" in the way some say is taking the Lord's name in vain. He would add expletives in between saying Jesus and Christ. He would say "Jesus (expletives) Christ" a lot. I would say it back to him when he said it and we both thought this was funny. Then we turned it into a contest. When we saw each other at work we would have to say Jesus (expletives + vulgar) Christ and with each time we would add more expletives and vulgar words to see who could outdo who. I thought this was the funniest thing.

Now that I was saved with the Holy Spirit dwelling in me and born again as a new creation, I could not form the Jesus (expletives + vulgar) Christ words with my tongue. I mean, my tongue literally could not physically form those words. I would get tongue-tied and it was just impossible to say those awful words. I was amazed! I would actually try hard to say cuss words and it was like someone locked my tongue from doing that. I just accepted the fact that I couldn't form those words out of my mouth anymore. It was like the Holy Spirit was keeping my tongue from doing that.

Of course, friends and co-workers took note that I did not cuss and say vulgar words anymore. When I was in a situation where it was expected to cuss and I didn't do it, I would be questioned if I was ok. My Jesus (expletive) Christ co-worker actually got angry with me after I would not join in on our private contest. These friends and co-workers would ask what's wrong with me and why did I change? I would tell them what happened, how Jesus saved me and healed me. Unfortunately, I lost friends because of this, and was labeled a 'radical Christian.'

Best Wednesday Service

Then the Holy Spirit put on my heart to go back to Holy Cross Lutheran church in Flushing, Michigan. This would be the first step, and the foundation for me, to start learning about God, His character, and who He is. I grew up attending Holy Cross Lutheran Church, and was confirmed there. I thought, maybe, I should go back to that church and get involved. I mean it's where I came from, right?

Somehow, I thought that Holy Cross had a Wednesday night service and I made plans to go that week. Wednesday came, and I remember being excited to go to the church service. Admittedly, I was a little nervous as I drove to the church because I haven't been there in years. I didn't know how anyone would react to seeing me, you know, because it's been a while. Would they accept me? Would they scold me for leaving for so long? I had no idea what to expect when I got there.

I drove into the parking lot and there were only two cars. My first thought was "am I early?" I looked at my watch and it was 6:57 so I wondered why there weren't more cars in the parking lot. I thought "maybe there is no service tonight." I sat in my car for a minute and then finally got up enough nerve to go inside and see if there was a service. I got out of my car and made my way into the church, and I was met by the Pastor's wife and the worship leader for the contemporary services. They smiled and seemed really happy to see me. They were wondering why I was there on a Wednesday night.

I said, "I thought you had service tonight".

Well obviously, there was no service, but God Almighty in His sovereignty took me there that night to meet with the Pastor's wife and the worship leader.

We made small talk for a while, and I told them what had happened to me, how God delivered me and healed my carpal tunnel. I told them I wanted to play bass for God Almighty. (Again, God knows what He is doing). They went on to explain that they are putting together songs for the upcoming Sunday contemporary service at Holy Cross. Guess what? Yup. They needed a bass player, and how about that- I just happened to play bass. They asked me to join the worship team. I said yes! I thought, Was this a coincidence? No. God's Sovereignty? Yes. Because God is in control. He of course, knew Holy Cross needed a bass player, He knew the time and place I would be saved and healed. His timing was perfect for me to wander into His church to start playing bass for Him and His glory.

That Sunday I ended up playing bass for Holy Cross Lutheran's contemporary service. It was definitely different from what I was used to. Playing clubs and venues was all about self-centered gratification. It was the idea of 'look at me, look what I can do'. Where playing bass in the church was about being selfless and giving the God Almighty honor and glory. I started to learn how to bring my gift to His altar and worship Him. Laying down my crown, humbling myself before Him.

After the service was done, I really had to try and put things in perspective. My hands were healed for this very reason. Which was to give Him the Glory through playing bass for Him. With this new perspective I was super excited to go down this journey of giving God the glory through playing bass. I realized that I was going to have to change my thinking when I played bass on Sunday morning. It was an opportunity to bring my flesh into submission. My flesh was used to always getting the glory when I would play. But thank God in His mercy that He would show me how to humble myself and give Him the Glory. I made it through that first service, and it would be the beginning of many, many, many services to come.

I Was Drawn to the Word

Right after joining the worship team at Holy Cross, I was drawn in my spirit to read the Word of God. I didn't know what to think about this so I thought I would get a hold of someone who I could talk to about reading God's Word. The first person who came to mind would be the Pastor of Holy Cross Lutheran Church. I figured he could help me understand what to do about reading the Word of God, after all, he is a Pastor.

I set an appointment with him, and the next day I went up to the church to meet with him. He remembered me from confirmation class and so we made small talk for a few minutes about being on the worship team and my parents.

Then he asked me, "How can I help you today?"

I said, "Pastor I have this weird desire to read the Bible and I am not sure what to think of it. Why all of a sudden can I not stop thinking about reading the Bible?"

He looked at me and smiled and said, "Mike, that's the Holy Spirit talking to you. He wants you to start reading the Bible."

I said, "Pastor, I am not a reader. I have a hard time comprehending what I read."

Pastor spent time encouraging me in that meeting that to know the will of God we are to read the Bible. He went on to explain that as Christians we learn all about God and His love for us by reading the Bible. This made sense to me that to understand God and how to know Him I should read the Bible. He prayed with me, and I left that meeting encouraged and excited to start reading about God.

Discouragement Arose

In the midst of my excitement to read the Bible my mind started to be flooded with thoughts of discouragement. They would come at me and say, "You're actually going to have to read Mike, you are not a reader." They would also say, "You will never understand it Mike, come on man, you've never finished reading a book." I started to doubt and be intimidated by the undertaking of reading the Bible. Realistically, I knew I was not much of a reader, never have been. I do not think that I ever finished a book in my life so reading to me was a laborious chore. I could read really well, I just had a hard time comprehending anything that I read. Nothing ever made sense to me. When I was in high school my mom tried to help me with my English classes by reading books to me with the idea that I would comprehend it. I was frustrated by that, and I am sure I said some things to my mom that were not good because I was frustrated. Sorry mom.

These intimidating thoughts kept me from starting to read the Bible because I had in my head that I wouldn't understand it anyway. Even though I was listening to the discouraging thoughts, the desire to read the Bible never went away. The Holy Spirit kept gently pushing me in my spirit to open the Bible and start reading. I kept telling myself I couldn't do it and I put up this fight, but the Holy Spirit was persistent and didn't give in. My desire to know God and read His word was becoming stronger each day. It was like the Holy Spirit knew that I was going to struggle with this, so He made sure to be gentle and understanding, yet persistent. That's what I felt from His side of this conversation. He was patient and waited for me to work this out in my spirit.

A few days go by, and I am looking through some boxes when I stumble across the Bible I used when I went through confirmation classes at Holy Cross. I would leave it out so I could see it because it just didn't feel right to put it back in the box I found it in. Every time I would walk by that Bible, I would think about reading it, but I was just so intimidated. A few more days would go by, and I would start picking it up and looking at it. There was just something about putting the Bible in my hands and bringing it closer to my being. It was like there was a sense of security and acceptance. I knew the Bible had something I needed, and it was like it was drawing me in to open it and start reading.

As this was happening, those negative thoughts would pop back up in my head. Then I would reason to myself there's no way I'll understand this book so I would set it back down and become discouraged. Back and forth and back and forth I would go- read it, or not? This was driving me crazy! It just seemed unattainable but yet it was right there calling me on to open the book and read. The Holy Spirit continued to be patient and gently encouraged me that I could do this. This battle within me would continue for days.

Then something happened. One day I found myself thumbing through that confirmation Bible. When I realized what I was doing, I thought, how did this happen? There was such a desire to be close to God and I knew in my spirit that reading the Bible would bring me closer to God. Physically touching it caused me to let go of my fear and intimidation. The next thing I knew I found myself reading the Bible in The Book of Psalms. It was as though all the bullying thoughts telling me I couldn't were finally silenced as I read. When I finished reading a passage from Psalms, I looked around the room. I couldn't believe it... to my amazement the Bible made sense to me. I was like "Wow! This isn't as bad as what I thought it would be. I really can do this." I have to say I was ecstatic over the fact that I could read it with ease, and it was clear. This was yet another huge hurdle to overcome. You could say that was a breakthrough for me, and all fear was gone. My confidence started to grow more and more as I read The Book of Psalms.

Ask For Wisdom

One day as I'm reading the Word, I was led by the Holy Spirit to read the book of James. Didn't really know what to expect when I started reading that book. Of course, I started reading chapter one, and when I got to verse 5, I just stopped in my tracks. It was like I couldn't move past this verse, and I just kept reading it over and over: *"If any of you lacks wisdom, let him ask God, who gives generously to all without reproach, and it will be given to him."* James 1:5 ESV

I said it out loud a few times "if anyone lacks wisdom, let him ask God, who gives generously to all without reproach, and it will be given to him." There is just something to be said when you speak something out loud. I thought to myself "I have knowledge, but I lack wisdom", then I thought "it said to ask God (pray), and then the promise of 'it' (wisdom) will be given to me."

In other words, God promises that if I ask for wisdom from His Word, then He will help me gain knowledge, which would lead to understanding, which would lead to gaining wisdom.

Now, the Holy Spirit was giving me this revelation, and I was fired up to ask God for wisdom like James 1:5 said to do. I just simply asked, "God, I'm asking for wisdom as I read Your Word, in Jesus Name, amen!" It was nothing fancy, and there wasn't a choir of angels singing, that I could hear anyway, no special light in the room. It was just a plain old practical prayer to God asking for something His Word says I can have. That was it! After I prayed, I started to read His Word again.

This was the first promise that God showed me in His Word. Thank you, Holy Spirit, for guiding me to this Bible verse. I would pray this prayer all the time. It became a habit before I would read the Word of God. This verse changed my life and helped me to gain the confidence I needed to read and believe Him for knowledge, understanding, and wisdom. I was amazed at what God was doing.

Funny Story

I found myself reading the Bible all the time. I just didn't want to put the book down. In my spirit I really felt like I needed some structure as to what to read in the Bible, I guess you could say I was looking for a Bible reading plan. I called Holy Cross and asked Pastor what I should read in the Bible. He was glad to help, and suggested that I read the 4 Gospels of the New Testament. I took his direction and prayed James 1:5 and started reading the Gospel of Matthew. It took me about a week to get through this Gospel. I was excited because I was able to understand what Jesus was actually saying.

After I got done reading the Gospel of Matthew, I started reading the Gospel of Mark. I noticed that it was saying pretty much the same thing as Matthew. I was kind of freaked out. Then I read the beginning of the Gospel of Luke and realized it pretty much said the same thing as the other two Gospels.

I thought the devil was doing some kind of trickery on me or something. Or maybe someone casted a spell on me.

I called Pastor and told him, "I'm under attack and need prayer immediately because the devil is tricking me and somehow making all the Gospels say the same thing."

I really thought I was being deceived by the devil. Pastor was gracious and calmly explained to me that I wasn't under attack. Then he went on to explain that the Gospels were 4 separate accounts of the life of Jesus, and between the four Gospels there will be accounts of His life that are the same and teachings repeated throughout. Needless to say, I was a little embarrassed, but it was, and still is, a good laugh for sure.

Thank God for Pastors in this world. They are the ones who tend to the sheep of the church. My Pastor, being Spirit-lead, was there to guide me and help me understand the Scriptures. His willingness to meet with me and not make me feel dumb for not knowing the Scriptures was crucial in the beginning of my journey of being a new creation. I could've very easily become frustrated and gave up on reading the Word. I could've justified it by saying that I am not a reader and will never understand it. But because of the Pastor's patience and encouragement along with the Holy Spirit's leading, I was able to push through that fear and intimidation.

Prophetic Word

As a newborn creation of God through the blood of Christ Jesus, I needed people to lead me in the way to go and tell me what is right and what is wrong, according to the Word of God. I found this in the leadership at Holy Cross. Those who were on the worship team had a passion for Jesus and were wanting to help me draw closer to God. It was wonderful being around such passionate brothers and sisters in Christ. We would have great conversations about the Word of God, and talk about things like prayer, trusting God, His amazing love, and what it meant to worship the King of Kings and Lord of Lords.

One week after a worship team rehearsal we were having a great conversation about the Lord. The worship leader grabbed my attention to tell me something. She looked right into my eyes and told me that I have the heart of an evangelist. I really didn't know what she meant at the time. I knew that an evangelist was one who called people on to salvation but had no idea how it all worked. I heard that Billy Graham was the greatest evangelist of our day. I thought maybe that's how it works. Tell people they need Jesus and to repent of their sin. This idea of calling people on to repent of their sin was very appealing to me. It felt natural. After she spoke this prophetic word over me, I would ponder this idea of being an evangelist often.

My church really emphasized the importance of reading the Scriptures correctly. Being a new believer, it was easy for me to misinterpret the Scriptures. That's why I am so thankful that God Almighty planted me at Holy Cross and surrounded me with good sound teachers of the Word of God. When I strayed with misinterpretations of Scriptures, they were right there to correct me. They instilled in me a saying that has helped me stay focused when I read the Word of God: *Let Scripture interpret Scripture.* Let the Word of God have the final say and do not take anything out of context. This would be the start of understanding that the Word of God was my final authority for my life.

CHAPTER 2
"Hear Me"

"Hear, O Lord, when I cry aloud; be gracious to me and answer me!"
Psalm 27:7 ESV

Winter/Spring 1992

The winter/Spring of 1992 was a very big and transitional time in my life. Right before the Lord healed me and saved me in March of that year my band Surreal came out with our first CD that January (1992). This was one of the most exciting things to happen to me in my life. It would be the first band project I was a part of that would complete a full-length recording studio CD project. Over the years I did a lot of work with my high school band. We would complete songs in the studio but never could get over the hump of putting out a finished product. Great music and solid execution but after our vocalist quit the band, we couldn't find one to fit what Craig was writing. Nothing bad against my high school band, we just did not have the resources to finish a complete project and press CDs.

When I got the call from Scott and Ben that the Surreal CDs were delivered and I could come get a box of CDs for myself, I was elated! This was in January of 1992, and I remember there was a lot of snow on the ground and the roads were bad, but I made my way over to Ben's place to get some CDs. I was beyond excited! The artwork looked great; the inside sleeve packet was put together wonderfully. The whole CD was a professional looking project. I had this feeling of accomplishment, and I was so proud of what we did as a band. I always dreamed of being on a professionally recorded CD and now I could say that I am a part of something like that.

First Song I Wrote with Lyrics

In the midst of all of it, the Surreal CD being released and my unbelievable experience of being saved and healed, the Lord gave me my first song with lyrics and melody. This was immediately after I was saved and healed (March of 1992). I really felt in my spirit that there was a song wanting to come out. Right after my carpal tunnel was healed, I started to pray to God to bless the music I was going to write and help me write lyrics. Lyrical ideas started to swirl around in my head. The swirling inside my spirit I recognized to be an answer to prayer and this was exciting for me.

Musically speaking the lyric writing that influenced me the most was very poetic and open-ended. Sure, there were the 'hair band' songs, but I was more into the lyrics of Led Zeppelin, Iron Maiden, Dio, Queensryche, and Kings X. These bands had lyrics that were hard for me to interpret but I loved listening to them. And the melodies were very emotional and engaging. I would ask myself how these songwriters would come up with these lyrics. I would read about their story behind the song and how they would be inspired emotionally to write what they wrote. This was very intimidating because I felt I didn't have any kind of emotion to pull from to write anything worthwhile. I didn't have a rough upbringing, I didn't really have any bad relationships, and I wasn't abused or on drugs or anything like that. My perception was that I didn't have a story or inspiration to pull from to write lyrics. I questioned how I was going to write something that had any meaning and interest at all.

Then the Holy Spirit reminded me that I have written and co-written music since I started playing bass at the age of 11. It wasn't like I could not write something musically. When I was 14, I wrote my very first guitar line. Even though I played bass in the band I was teaching myself guitar as well. The chord progression I wrote was a descending progression starting with an Em chord walking down with D and C to a B7 chord. My high school band and I turned this into a ballad. Then when I was a senior in high school, I wrote a descending progression on my bass. Key of Bm natural minor. This was the first time that a melody came to me while playing the progression on my bass. In my head it was a violin melody but nonetheless it was a melody. When I played the progression, I would hum the melody so I wouldn't forget it. Both of these progressions would end up being used on future projects.

Because I never wrote any lyrics I felt as though I wouldn't be any good at it. There was just a fear and a lack of confidence because I never put in the time to work on putting lyrics to music. This to me was like jumping off the diving board for the first time when I was 7 years old. My parents enrolled me into swim lessons over the summer. One of the things I had to do was jump off a diving board into the deep end. The swim instructor was right there to get me after I jumped in. But I was petrified to do this. The fear of the unknown and I thought what if I drowned. I would go to the edge of the diving board and then get scared and go back. This would happen several times. I just couldn't jump off because of all the things that were going through my mind that could go wrong. The biggest thing I was scared of is I didn't know how to swim yet. The instructor promised me she would safely bring me to the shallow end after I dived in. I just couldn't do it.

Eventually, after a few days of going to the edge of the diving board I made up my mind that I was going to jump in. Determined, I went to the edge of the diving board, took a deep breath, and just went for it and jumped in. After my swim instructor brought me to safety, I wanted to jump off that diving board all the time. It was just that first-time fear in doing it that I had to overcome. It was the same idea with writing lyrics, I just had to jump in and trust that God would help me do this. I really wanted to write lyrics that were God-centered.

Verse One

The next day I started to get words that would just come to my mind. It seemed weird at first, as the words would be inside my mind, so I thought I would just write down what my mind was saying. I didn't even know if what I was writing made any sense. I was hesitant at first because this was something new to me. I assumed that maybe I was writing lyrics. I wasn't too sure if this is how lyric writing worked. I just decided to go with the flow and trust the process. Going with the flow by just writing down what's coming to me and then trusting the process that I can do lyrical edits after I write them down. Here is the first lyrical verse I ever wrote.

Time stands still empty faces
Dreams are gone there's no traces
Fear moves on through the night
Peace is gone is this wrong

This verse came from the idea of the world being devastated by something. I had a vision of a world that looked like it was destroyed by nuclear war. Because of this it created fear throughout for those who were left, and peace was nowhere to be found. Which describes the condition of the human heart severed by sin. Where all seems lost and there is no hope.

Then came verse two. I just wrote down what came to my mind:
Is there a way to find an answer
I look at this cross and I see
He died for all of us and washed away all my sin, all my sin

I wanted to show these lyrics to someone, so the first person I showed them to was Regine. Yes, I wanted her approval because I was nervous as to whether the lyrics were any good.

I called her up and told her I had some lyrics that I wanted to show her, so she told me to come over. I immediately went over to her host parents' house. I remember being in the kitchen as I was showing her these lyrics. I was nervously excited and was looking for her response.

As I watched her read them, I asked, "Well what do you think?"

She looked at me and said, "These lyrics are good," and gave me the green light to keep going and finish the song. I was overwhelmed with joy that she liked them.

I asked her to join in and help write some lyrics to this song. She was hesitant at first but then the next thing I know she joined in on the lyric writing and added the first two lines to the second verse – *'I'm crying out fearful thoughts, Powerless movements with no results.'* Those two lyric lines resonated with my spirit, so I put them in front of the second verse I wrote. The lyrics read like this.

Time stands still empty faces
Dreams are gone there's no traces
Fear moves on through the night
Peace is gone, is this wrong?
I'm crying out fearful thoughts
Powerless movements with no results
Is there a way to find an answer
I look at this cross and I see
He died for all of us and washed away all my sin, all my sin

The two lyric lines that she wrote, *'I'm crying out fearful thoughts - Powerless movements with no results,'* have the meaning that we can do nothing to obtain salvation within ourselves. Only God Almighty has the capability and power to save us. With that in mind, it went perfectly to the next lyric of *'Is there a way to find an answer.'* As I had just spent several months before I was saved searching for answers. In my thought process I tried many things within my own strength, thinking within my own power,

I could obtain salvation on my own.

The next two lines now become more impactful because the answer I found is in Christ Jesus and the work of the cross - *'I look at the cross and I see He died for all of us and washed away all my sins'.* Simple and to the point. This lyric came from my experience when I realized that Christ Jesus saved me and healed me. He took away my shame and guilt and reconciled me to himself. Even though I went to Him feeling shameful, I walked away knowing I am forgiven.

Then came the chorus of the song. I started to hear a lyric in my head *'Can You hear, hear me calling your Name'*. This lyric came from when I cried out for mercy to God and begged Him to help me after I realized that I needed a Savior. With this line of thinking, the chorus became a prayer to God to hear me as I called out to Him and repented of my sin after realizing I am lost and dead without Him. From that lyric I came up with the title "Can You Hear." It made sense because the first line of the chorus has those words, but eventually the song ended up with the title of "Hear Me." Here are the original lyrics to the chorus.

Can You hear, hear me calling your Name
I drop down to my knees, I feel so ashamed
Can You hear, hear me calling to You
Oh Lord hear me please, tell me what to do

I worked on these lyrics coming up with melody and music. During the verse, I ended up using a descending chord progression of Em - D - Cmaj7 for those of you who are musicians. It was kind of nerve racking at first trying to come up with a melody. I tried a few ideas, and at first I couldn't tell if the melody ideas were worth working on. Then I just kept at it, going with the flow and trusting the process. Eventually, a melody started to come about naturally and seemed to fit the guitar line.

I really like songs with anthem choruses so the chorus in this song ended up being very anthem-like. I applied my music theory knowledge to write the chord progression to the chorus. I made sure it was progressive and not retrogressive. There are certain chord movements that are considered strong moves and others chord movements are considered weak. I used the progressive approach to write the chord progression in the chorus. This is the progression for the chorus- Em-(f#)G-C-(b)Am-G(f#) back to Em.

A few days later I took this song to my best friend Micah. Micah was my music writing partner back then. He thought the song was really good and wanted to add a third verse to it. I had a lot of respect for Micah as a musician and songwriter so I left the lyrics I wrote with him for a few days to see what he could come up with. The next day he gave me a call to stop by and check out what he came up with. The lyrics and melody he wrote were amazing and fit perfectly with the direction of the song.

My heart finds home again
In the Valley where we began
On the mountain side I see the Lamb of God
Roaming through the pastures of the lives He's saved
He speaks to me, now I know what to do, now I know what to do

While I was reading the lyrics he wrote, I just had a sense of God's love. I asked Micah to tell me what these lyrics meant. He said, "*My heart finds home again, In the Valley where we began*" is going back home to God. He explained how Adam and Eve had a relationship with God before sin entered the world and severed that relationship. 'Going back to the Valley' meant the Garden of Eden when there was a relationship with God that was one-on-one. He went on to explain that he had a vision of Jesus "*on the mountain side I see the Lamb of God, roaming through the pastures of the lives He saved.*" I just had a sense of God's mercy and grace because these lyrics were describing what I just recently went through. This lyric is also a great description of Ezekiel 34 when God says He Himself will tend the flock and go find the sheep that have been scattered along the mountainside. Ezekiel 34:13

ESV - *"And I will bring them out from the peoples and gather them from the countries, and will bring them to their own land; I will feed them on the mountains of Israel, in the valleys and in all the inhabited places of the country."*

Even though it was a collaborative effort I still consider it the first song I wrote lyrics to. The Holy Spirit put on my heart what to write and used Micah and Regine to help lyrically finish the song. I was so excited to complete the song as a whole. I would play it and sing it on my acoustic every day. Micah eventually learned the song and we wanted to record it in the studio. We started to record this song a few months later at The Disc recording studio but never finished it. In 2017 I finally was able to record this song on my Threefold Mercy project called "My Hope Is In You". I wish Micah was here to celebrate that moment with me. Rest in Heaven Micah.

"Hear Me"
Time stands still empty faces
Dreams are gone there's no traces
Fear moves on through the night
Peace is gone is this wrong
I'm crying out fearful thoughts
Powerless movements with no results
Is there a way to find an answer
I look at this cross and I see
He died for all of us, and washed away my sin
He died for all of us, and washed away
All my sin
Can You hear, hear me calling your Name
I drop down to my knees, I feel so ashamed
Can You hear, hear me calling to You
Oh Lord hear me please, tell me what to do
My heart finds home again
In the Valley where we began
On the mountain side I see the Lamb of God
Roaming through the pastures of the lives He's saved

He speaks to me, now I know what to do
Now I know what to do
Can You hear, hear me calling your Name
I drop down to my knees, I feel so ashamed
Can You hear, hear me calling to You
Oh Lord hear me please, tell me what to do

The song is me crying out to Him for mercy and wanting to know His Love for me and receive the free gift of grace. The verses are me realizing that I am in need of a Savior and the chorus was my heart wanting to be in the family of God. As I approached His throne of grace in the bowling alley, I cried out to Him, I did receive mercy and grace in my time of need. Then He made it clear what I was supposed to do by healing my carpal tunnel and wanting to proclaim Christ Crucified through music and preaching of His Word. This song was in His perfect time to set the foundation for things to come.

The Heart of God-The Lost

As I would work on making the arrangement of "Hear Me" better, I would find myself drawing closer to the heart of God. The lyrics started to have deeper meaning and it was like I was being pulled to have an understanding of the knowledge of what the Holy Spirit inspired me to write. Singing the song over and over to iron out the wrinkles just made me realize that God's heart is to save that which is lost. I was lost at one point. In the kingdom of darkness and blinded by the deception of Satan. I realized that the people of this earth were God's creation, and His heart is to restore His creation to Himself.

That is why Jesus had to come into this world. To save that which is lost, that being the human race. I realized before that I was lost but this time it was different. It was now becoming a conviction in my heart. I thought about what it was like when I was lost. I had a visual of being lost deep within a forest with no idea how to get out. While I had this visual going through my mind, I could feel the anxiety of being lost. I had no idea where to start, where to go, what direction to start walking. In this visual I tried everything to find my way out but had no success. I tried to put together a map in my head to get me out of this forest which gave me a sliver of hope, but still, no success getting out. It didn't matter what I did or said, I was lost with no hope.

The feeling of knowing I was lost is something I will never forget. The devil was the one who kept blinding me and deceiving me to keep me in this place of darkness feeling lost with no hope. Then I came across this Scripture in Revelation 12 *"Then the dragon became furious with the woman and went off to make war on the rest of her offspring, on those who keep the commandments of God and hold to the testimony of Jesus. And he stood on the sand of the sea."* Revelation 12:17 ESV . This verse opened my eyes, and I realized that the devil hates me simply because I am a creation of the Almighty God. And because of this hate for me, he is making war against me.

All that time growing up I was deceived to think that God was the one bullying me. In reality it was the devil bullying me. It was him who was deceiving me to think that everything good was bad and everything bad was good. The devil doesn't care about me; he just wanted me to stay in that darkness just to spite God. The devil could care less what kind of suffering I was going through. He wasn't there to help me when I was down. He would kick me to keep me down. He didn't care if I was lonely or sad or being made fun of. Why? Because he hates me and is making war against me.

Now I became angry at the devil for oppressing me all those years and making me think it was God Almighty doing it to me. I had blamed God for attacking me and trying to make me subscribe to a way of thinking that supposedly repressed my freedoms. The devil twisted the truth and turned me against God with his lies and deception. I searched for the answers and eventually ended up at the foot of the cross asking My Savior for mercy. Thank God He heard that prayer and pursued me. I was lost, but now I am found, all because of God's love, mercy and grace.

When this was going on I just happened to be reading the Gospels. In Luke 15, Jesus talks about the lost sheep, the lost coin, and the prodigal son. *"Now the tax collectors and sinners were all drawing near to hear him. And the Pharisees and the scribes grumbled, saying, "This man receives sinners and eats with them." So he told them this parable: "What man of you, having a hundred sheep, if he has lost one of them, does not leave the ninety-nine in the open country, and go after the one that is lost, until he finds it? And when he has found it, he lays it on his shoulders, rejoicing. And when he comes home, he calls together his friends and his neighbors, saying to them, 'Rejoice with me, for I have found my sheep that was lost.' Just so, I tell you, there will be more joy in heaven over one sinner who repents than over ninety-nine righteous persons who need no repentance. "Or what woman, having ten silver coins, if she loses one coin, does not light a lamp and sweep the house and seek diligently until she finds it? And when she has found it, she calls together her friends and neighbors, saying, 'Rejoice with me, for I have found the coin that I had lost.' Just so, I tell you, there is joy before the angels of God over one sinner who repents." And he said, "There was a man who had two sons. And the younger of them said to his father, 'Father, give me the share of property that is coming to me.' And he divided his property between them. Not many days later, the younger son gathered all he had and took a journey into a far country, and there he squandered his property in reckless living. And when he had spent everything, a severe famine arose in that country, and he began to be in need. So he went and hired himself out to one of the citizens of that country, who sent him into his fields to feed pigs. And he was longing to be fed with the pods that the pigs ate, and no one gave him anything. "But when he came to himself, he said, 'How many of my father's hired servants have more than enough bread, but I perish here with hunger! I will arise and go to my father, and I will say to him, "Father, I have sinned against heaven and before you. I am no longer worthy to be called your son. Treat me as one of your hired servants."' And he arose and came to his father. But* while he was still a long way off, his father saw him and felt compassion, and ran and embraced him and kissed him. And the son said to him, 'Father, I have sinned against heaven and before you. I am no longer worthy to be called your son.' But the father said to his servants, 'Bring quickly the best robe, and put it on him, and put a ring on his hand, and shoes on his feet. And bring the fattened calf and kill it, and let us eat and celebrate. For this my son was dead, and is alive again; he was lost, and is found.' And they began to celebrate. "Now his older son was in the field, and as he came and drew near to the house, he heard music and dancing. And he called one of the servants and asked what these things meant. And he said to him, 'Your brother has come, and your father has killed the fattened calf, because he has received him back safe and sound.' But he was angry and refused to go in. His father came out and entreated him, but he answered his father, 'Look, these many years I have served you, and I never disobeyed your command, yet you never gave me a young goat, that I might celebrate with my friends. But when this son of yours came, who has devoured your property with prostitutes, you killed the fattened calf for him!' And he said to him, 'Son, you are always with me, and all that is mine is yours. It was fitting to celebrate and be glad, for this your brother was dead, and is alive; he was lost, and is found.'"" Luke 15:1-32 ESV

Parable Revelation

There were many things that stuck out to me in these 3 parables as I was trying to grasp what the Holy Spirit was trying to get me to understand. The first thing was the Shepherd and the woman both pursued what was lost, which was the sheep and the coin. The shepherd would 'go after' and the woman would 'diligently seek' until what was lost was found. In light of that, I couldn't help but to think about how God Almighty came after me, pursued me, and pulled me out of the deception of darkness to put me into the kingdom of His Light.

Another thing that stuck out was that they both say that there is joy in heaven over one sinner who repents. I was able to reflect on what happened in heaven the night I was saved and healed in the pool hall of that bowling alley. If God's Word is true, which I believe it is, then there was joy in heaven that night because I turned from my sin and fixed my eyes on Jesus. I had to think about this for a while to really understand what this meant for me. I would envision thousands upon thousands of angels rejoicing because I was brought into the family of God after I repented. This brought a sense of approval not only from the angels of heaven but also from my Father in Heaven.

The parable of the prodigal son has so much in it to learn from, but at that time in my life, I simply remembered that the son was lost and now he is found. Also, how he was squandering his money and partying and then realized he made a mistake and wanted to go home. That is similar to what happened to me. With all the self-centered living I was doing, it came to a point that I realized I needed to be with God the Father. I thought a lot about how the father of the prodigal son welcomed him back home without any hesitation. That must have been how the Father welcomed me back home when I repented of my sin.

This understanding that the Holy Spirit had given me made the hymn "Amazing Grace" so much more meaningful. The popular verse that everyone knows, even unbelievers: *"Amazing grace! How sweet the sound, that saved a wretch like me. I once was lost, but now am found; was blind, but now I see."*

This was one of many favorite hymns that my dad would love to sing in church. When hymns were sung in church, I would grab a hymnal and try to sing along with him. He would always belt out those hymns like he owned them. It was always so much fun doing this with my dad. Trying to keep up with him was a task that's for sure. Now that I was going to church again, this would become a common thing that we would do, when I was not playing bass on the worship team during service.

The song "Hear Me" would become a foundation in my life to spring from, as I began to understand what the Gospel is and how God could love a wretch like me. I would continue to ponder in my heart this idea that I was once lost and now I am found. How heaven rejoiced when I repented and turned to God the Father. It was the beginning of developing a heart for the lost and a desire to see the lies of the devil destroyed over people's lives. I wanted those around me set free from a feeling of no hope, and come to know the love of Christ Jesus.

CHAPTER 3
"Building Confidence"

"And this is the confidence that we have toward him, that if we ask anything according to his will he hears us." 1 John 5:14 ESV

Prayer

During this time, I was reading a lot of the Word of God and as I read it I started to have this strong desire to learn how to pray. I've always been intimidated to approach God and pray. I was always afraid I would stumble over my words and say something wrong. Or it wouldn't make sense to God. I wondered if it is ok to ask for things for myself, or should it always be for others. I really didn't know. I did know this though, God Almighty answered my prayer when I cried out for mercy before I was saved. I knew God hears our prayers. I just wanted to know how to do it on a daily basis like the Bible was telling me to do.

Growing up, I was taught in Sunday school that I could pray to God like I was having a conversation with Him. I remember my dad would pray at dinnertime. I remembered seeing and hearing in his voice a reverence for God when he would pray at home. But the biggest thing that caught my attention about prayer was when both my parents would come back to their seats after receiving communion and take a moment to pray. I could tell my dad was having an intense moment with God by his facial expressions. I always wondered what they prayed about. It seemed like a time of cleansing when I would watch them pray. This would be a seed planted by the Holy Spirit to start teaching me the importance of prayer according to the Word of God.

As I got older, I had a habit of praying when something bad happened to me or someone I loved. It was like I would pray to God only when I needed Him.
In light of this, I thought about how when I was 15 and my dad fell through the ceiling of the garage. He went headfirst into the hood of the parked car in the garage. I saw him plunge into the car hood and bounce off of it. There was an instant rush of anxiety that filled my body, and I freaked out and I didn't know what to do. He was on the floor after bouncing off the hood of the car, so I pulled him off the floor and helped him into the other car in the garage right next to us. He was in so much pain. I ran into the house to get my mom so we could get him some help.

I'll never forget the car ride to the hospital. When we were driving him there, I remember praying like crazy. I was practically begging God to not let him die. That's what came to my mind to pray. I was praying in the moment where there was a lot of anxiety and all I knew is I wanted to see my dad fixed and healed.

We got my dad to the hospital, and they were able to find out what he had broken and got him some pain meds. He broke his back and messed up his neck pretty badly. Doctors said he was lucky that the car was parked below him because the hood of the car absorbed the impact when he fell.

When my dad fell through that ceiling, I became a prayer chatterbox. I was praying for things like I knew what I was doing. I really had no relationship with God and wondered why He would answer my prayers. After all, I was into music that glorified Satan, I had a bad attitude towards God, and saw Him as the oppressive enemy. And yet, God Almighty in His sovereignty saved my dad's life that night, and I am more than thankful for that. His love and mercy are amazing.

Rejecting Occult

After I was saved, I rejected all occult activity from my past and any leftover occult thinking in my life. I was already shown in Scriptures that witchcraft is an abomination to the Lord and is considered rebellion towards the Lord. *"Let no one be found among you who sacrifices their son or daughter in the fire, who practices divination or sorcery, interprets omens, engages in witchcraft, or casts spells, or who is a medium or spiritist or who consults the dead. Anyone who does these things is detestable to the Lord; because of these same detestable practices the Lord your God will drive out those nations before you. You must be blameless before the Lord your God."* Deuteronomy 18:10-13 NIV

Because the occult was rooted well into my being throughout my teen years, it had to be uprooted. I realized within the first week of being saved that there is no way that the Holy Spirit and the occult-mindset could co-exist. One is for God, and the other is against God. When I was desiring witchcraft and spell-casting as a teenager, I knew it went against God and His kingdom. The two are completely opposite to each other. I never saw the two, God and Satan, as being equal. I always knew that God was stronger and there was no way that Satan could overpower God.

Satan's deception is powerful. Even though I was brought up in the church and had a solid Sunday school teaching, I was still deceived. Satan had been planting seed in me from an early age, right along with the Plowman of the Holy Spirit; creating within me desires to rebel against God and to be a witch. No spirit-filled follower of Christ Jesus can desire to be a witch. That would be like trying to mix oil and water. The two will separate and never allow the other to become a part of their being.

The Holy Spirit made it very clear that I was to have nothing to do with witchcraft, sorcery, spell casting or any kind of divination. I was to purge it out of my life and reject it. When Christ Crucified was preached after Christ Jesus' ascension, we see those who practiced witchcraft rejecting it as well. *"And a number of those who had practiced magic arts brought their books*

together and burned them in the sight of all. And they counted the value of them and found it came to fifty thousand pieces of silver. So the word of the Lord continued to increase and prevail mightily."
Acts 19:19-20 ESV

It was a no brainer for me to reject the occult ideology and no longer subscribe to that way of thinking. I wasn't sure how to do this. I didn't know if I should go to my Pastor and ask for prayer or what. I decided I would pray to God Almighty, the Lord of Hosts, and asked Him to purge this ideology out of me. To give me no desire to pray to Satan but instead that my desire would be to burn for the Lord Jesus Christ. I asked that He uproot any and all of the seeds that took root in me from my past. I asked that His angels come to protect me and minister to me. While praying this I could actually feel and sense something happening around me. I already knew that the spirit realm was real so it wasn't anything alarming. I did, however, sense a deeper connection with God Almighty as I prayed that way. It is my first recollection of doing a form of spiritual warfare prayer.

Praying For Others

As this idea of self-centered prayer was being uprooted from me the Holy Spirit put a burning desire inside of me to pray for others. I really didn't know what I should pray for other people. I mean, should I pray for their needs to be met? In my mind it seemed like that would be the same as praying self-centered prayers. Praying for someone else's self-centered request didn't make sense. I asked myself what do other people really need?

I made a list of people who I wanted to pray for. As I looked at this list, I would ask what each person specifically needed. It seemed all I could come up with was a self-centered need. New job, better finances, more friends, that they would be healed, send them a spouse, and so forth. It all seemed like things to make their life better than what it was. These were all things a witch would cast a spell for, or Satan would want you to pray for. It seemed like they would be prayers of discontentment. None of this set well with me.

Then it dawned on me that I could ask for wisdom, like James 1:5 says, as to what to pray for others. I prayed that God would help me understand what I should be praying for others on a daily basis. The Holy Spirit made it very clear to pray that they come to know God the Father's love, mercy, and grace, which is Ephesians 2:4-5. This is what Regine prayed for me all the time before I was saved. Now this was something that felt right in my spirit. Praying for others to draw closer to God Almighty and for their salvation made sense. Because I realized that salvation is really what we all need. **All the material things and self-advancement in life comes and goes and does nothing to seal an unbeliever in the Holy Spirit with the blessed hope of salvation.**

Agape love is a love where you give the person what they need, not what they want. What every creation of Elohim needs is salvation for the forgiveness of sins. No human will ever want this salvation because we are separated from God and dead in our sin. The sinful nature will never want anything to do with God Almighty. But, by the power of the Holy Spirit and preaching of the Word of God, the faith for salvation can be obtained. I also started to pray that each person on my list would come to know Christ Crucified and the forgiveness of sin. I would pray that each person would be taken out of the kingdom of darkness and put into the Kingdom of light. I would pray that each person would no longer be blinded and deceived by Satan and that their eyes would be open to the gospel of Christ Jesus. This was the beginning for me to learn how to pray according to what the Bible says.

Praying for Myself

As I was learning how to pray for others, the idea of how to pray for myself came back to my spirit. As I posed the question, "What am I supposed to pray for myself?" the Lord put this in my spirit: *Pray to be closer to God Almighty's heart.* Then the Holy Spirit took me to the Scripture Psalm 19:12-14 to pray for myself. *"Who can discern his errors? Declare me innocent from hidden faults. Keep back your servant also from presumptuous sins; let them not have dominion over me! Then I shall be blameless, and innocent of great transgression. Let the words of my mouth and the meditation of my heart be acceptable in your sight, O Lord, my rock and my redeemer."* Psalm 19:12-14 ESV. My prayer for myself became to not allow sin to dominate my life again. This was such a huge revelation for me. Sin separated me as an unbeliever, and I didn't want it to hinder me with my walk with the Lord. I would pray this every day for myself.

One of the members on the worship team also gave me some insight on how to pray. Knowing where I was at, this person took me to the Scriptures:*""And when you pray, you must not be like the hypocrites. For they love to stand and pray in the synagogues and at the street corners, that they may be seen by others. Truly, I say to you, they have received their reward. But when you pray, go into your room and shut the door and pray to your Father who is in secret. And your Father who sees in secret will reward you. And when you pray, do not heap up empty phrases as the Gentiles do, for they think that they will be heard for their many words. Do not be like them, for your Father knows what you need before you ask him. Pray then like this: "Our Father in heaven, hallowed be your name. Your kingdom come, your will be done, on earth as it is in heaven. Give us this day our daily bread, and forgive us our debts, as we also have forgiven our debtors. And lead us not into temptation, but deliver us from evil."* Matthew 6:5-13 ESV. This simply showed me a pattern to follow when I pray. Acknowledge the Father, forgiveness for me and others, and keep me from anything evil. This broke any kind of idea that I had to use all these eloquent-type prayers with all these biblical words.

I would end up writing down this pattern so I would have prayer direction when I prayed. Now I had a list of people to pray for and a pattern to follow as well. This was important for me to have because it would help me develop a habit of prayer and I would be able to stay focused and on target with what I was praying for. I found myself also writing specific things I was praying for others and myself in relation to salvation and keeping sin at bay. This way I could also see when and how God would answer my prayers.

Group Prayer

As I was developing a personal prayer life, I was still having confidence issues praying out loud within a group. Being on the worship team, I would have many chances every week to pray in a group setting. We would always pray as a group before and after each rehearsal. We would chat a little bit about what was going on in our lives and see if anyone had any prayer requests. Then members of the group would volunteer to pray for the needs that were talked about. This would bring about a sense of community and unity within our group.

Group prayer at my church is where we would all hold hands in a circle, and someone would start praying out loud. Then when that person was done, the person to their right would start praying. If you did not want to pray out loud you would squeeze the hand of the person to your right. It was made clear that if you did not pray out loud there would be no condemnation for doing so. No explanation as to why you would not pray. I would squeeze the hand of the person to my right all the time because I did not feel ready or comfortable praying out loud yet.

The other worship team members seemed to know what to say and were so fluent when they prayed. They would pray with so much love and confidence towards God and quote Scriptures as they prayed. I kept comparing myself to them and told myself that I did not sound like them. This was intimidating. That was a lot of pressure for me to handle because

I didn't have the Scriptural lingo down and didn't have verses memorized. I was afraid of sounding like a fool, and didn't want to do it wrong. This would really tear me up inside. On my way home, I would think about what I could've prayed and then I would beat myself up for not praying out loud. I obviously prayed out loud by myself but for some reason I couldn't get over the hump in group prayer.

Pray The Scriptures

Then the Holy Spirit pressed on my heart to pray the Scriptures. He just showed me not too long ago that I am to pray through the Scriptures in my personal prayer time. This was a little different though as He wanted me to memorize the passage of a Scripture and pray it out loud. This made total sense to me. I ended up talking to fellow worship team members about it and they confirmed that it was always a good idea to pray the Scriptures.

During this time, I noticed that Apostle Paul wrote prayers in his letters to the churches. I figured I would start with his prayers for the church. The Scriptures I focused on first was in the book of Ephesians: *"that the God of our Lord Jesus Christ, the Father of glory, may give you the Spirit of wisdom and of revelation in the knowledge of him, having the eyes of your hearts enlightened, that you may know what is the hope to which he has called you, what are the riches of his glorious inheritance in the saints, and what is the immeasurable greatness of his power toward us who believe, according to the working of his great might."* Ephesians 1:17-19 ESV. What I would do is hand write this out so I could keep it in my pocket and then pull it out when I needed help memorizing it. This would go on for a while but eventually I was able to memorize the whole passage.

It came time to join in on the worship team prayer time. The circle started to pray, then it came to my turn. I opened my mouth and prayed this passage out loud replacing the word 'you' with the word 'us'. That would mean I was praying this Scripture over us as a worship team. Once I got going it was hard to shut me up. After that day I had to find balance and learn not to be long-winded. I was finally able to pray within a group and overcome my fear of looking dumb. Man, I felt like I conquered a mountain and broke through a barrier. I was gaining the confidence that I could pray for anything.

Becoming A Leader

I was going through a lot at this time in my life. I knew that my bass playing was getting stronger every day after it was healed by Christ Jesus, but now I was facing the beginning stages of how to be a leader. Thoughts would flood my brain everyday like, *"You can't do this,"* *"no one will like your music,"* and *"you will fail and crumble under pressure."* I found that those negative thoughts were not too bad to push through. I just had to believe that this music was inspired by the Holy Spirit, and not worry about what others thought or said.

I think the biggest concern of mine though was that I didn't want to frustrate those involved with this project and have them see me as an incompetent leader. Being indecisive can make those trying to follow my lead lose confidence in me as a leader. I just couldn't deal with the thought of that. Everyone has always complimented me for being an exceptional bass player, so I was used to being accepted and looked up to. Now, I was putting myself in a very vulnerable position. I had to learn to make decisions even if it wasn't the one that everyone was happy with.

I prayed for wisdom and strength to get this music that Regine and I were working on recorded in the studio before she went back to Germany. This was always the goal of why she and I initially were getting together. It was an exciting time in my life because it would be the first project that I was the main songwriter on with the vision of what the music would be like.

Along with that, I had to be the leader and carry all the weight of this project and make all the decisions as to whether the execution of parts in the studio were good enough, among other things. This is something I've always wanted to do, and I guess there was no better time than the present.

Practice Begins

I ended up booking time at the Disc Ltd in Detroit, Michigan. I just happened to know a great guitar player from college, and he just happened to know a great drummer who lived in the area. They both agreed to work with me on these songs that Regine and I were working on. It was great to find them so quickly because we were on a time schedule with Regine leaving in a few months. I gave them cassettes of the demo ideas I recorded on my cassette deck at home, and we set a date for our first rehearsal.

While driving to the first rehearsal it was a snowy, rainy, foggy night, and I was calming my mind down from the business of the day. When I got out of my car, I remember the quiet of the night. Soothing and peaceful. I walked into the house, and there was a welcoming smell of coffee and home cooked meals. We made our way to the room to rehearse, the lights were dimmed, and we made quiet chatter about the day as I set up.

We were ready to rehearse, and I thought we could start with the song called "What Has Come of Me." The drummer counted it in, and we started to play the song. About 5 seconds in I could not believe what was happening. I was actually hearing my song with guitar and drums, and it was blowing me away. This would be the first time I would hear a song I wrote in my head being played by skilled musicians. What an amazing feeling and experience!

I have never played with a drummer like this one. Shorter kinda guy, but when he sat down on those drums he was like an intense crazy man. He is the only one that could make his piccolo snare drum crack at an ear-piercing volume every time he hit it. He definitely took a lot of pride in that.

Studio Day

The day to record the bed tracks of this music had arrived. We got loaded in and had all our gear set up and mic'd. We decided to start out with the song 'What Has Come of Me'. Our engineer got a great mix in the headphones and away we went. It only took a few tries to get that song down to our liking and recorded. This was a huge success because back in the 1990's there was no such thing as free studio time or buying a studio to record at home for the average consumer. If time was wasted that would mean money wasted. There were two other songs we recorded where classical technique and skill on the guitar was needed. A song called "Sing It For Me Now" and the song I just finished writing with Micah and Regine, "Hear Me". The last two songs highlighted for this project was a song called "Liquid Eclipse," which is the one I wrote my senior year in high school, and a duet version of the classical piece "Ava Maria."

Recording the song "Liquid Eclipse" was definitely exciting for me, being it was my first song I wrote on bass. When I was in college, music theory classes were required as a declared music major. My second semester during freshman year, we had to write a music piece using choral writing and music theory as our guide. I decided to use the song "Liquid Eclipse." Mind you I already had the descending progression written but I had to make it into a four-part choral piece. After I wrote the arpeggiated chord progression out on staff paper, I had to write out the melody that I always hummed in my head, which ended up being the violin part. I sat at a piano and figured the notes out and put that on the staff paper. The next thing I know I had written my first song for bass on staff paper in choral format. I gave this piece of music to Regine so she could read the violin part. Of course, she made suggestions for melody from a violinist perspective. They were good ideas and we incorporated them into the song.

When I started to work on this song with Regine, I wanted to extend it beyond what I originally wrote and give it lyrics. I saw that song as the death of Jesus Christ and the moments he hung on the cross. I turned it into being like a scene from a movie with all the background sounds going on. The people in distress and the hammering of the nails into His hands and feet. I also wanted to capture the Scripture of someone saying what Jesus's last words were *"And about the ninth hour Jesus cried out with a loud voice, saying, "Eli, Eli, lema sabachthani?" that is, "My God, my God, why have you forsaken me?" And Jesus cried out again with a loud voice and yielded up his spirit."* Matthew 27:46, 50 ESV. We wrote another movement to try and capture this idea of Jesus' death on the cross.

Tough Decision

We were finally ready to start cutting some scratch vocals on the songs. At the last-minute, Micah and I came up with this idea of making the second-half of the song "Liquid Eclipse" into a storytelling spoken word. Like a common city peasant telling the story from his perspective of this man Jesus and what happened with him dying on the cross. I thought it was a cool idea in my head. We went to record the idea.

While we were recording this idea the guitar player and drummer just happened to be there during that time and I could tell they were concerned about something. The guitar player came to talk to me about how there was a wide spectrum of styles of music going from a pretty guitar line to a hard progressive song. He wanted to see me cut the soft songs and be hard progressive only. I told them I wasn't going to do that. Then he and the drummer talked privately for a few minutes while I was trying to focus on what Micah was trying to do with this song. Next thing I know they came out of the room they were in and wanted to talk to me. They decided to talk to me right in front of everyone and basically gave me an ultimatum on the spot. They said if I didn't get rid of the soft songs and replace Micah as a singer then they would quit. My first thought was "What the heck?!" Then I looked at them and without hesitation I told them they would have to quit. This was an unpopular decision to make but I had to as the leader.

They started packing up their stuff. I told the others to take a break. I shook their hand and thanked them for their hard work, then Micah and I, along with a few others, helped both of them carry their gear down the stairs and load it up in their car. Now that the band was pretty much dismantled, Micah was wondering if we should keep recording. I told Micah that we need to finish what we started. I gathered everyone together and we had a moment of prayer, encouraging one another, and finished out that night in the studio.

CHAPTER 4
"The Year of Transitions"

"I will instruct you and teach you in the way you should go; I will counsel you with my eye upon you." Psalm 32:8 ESV

Summer/Fall of 1992

It was now July, and time for Regine to go back to her native land of Germany. Such a trooper she was. It was two nights before she had to leave so I took her to the first place we went out to way back in the fall. We talked about all the things we did together. Hanging out at the Disc, going to Surreal rehearsals, and shooting a lot of pool. One thing that we talked about is how there was never any drama between us. I remember that very clearly. There always seemed to be peace between us. Once and a while I would get out of line, and she would bring me back in line. It was good for us to recap and ponder our time together before she left. We also had to recognize what God had done the last 11 months while she was here in America. Many things to be thankful for and we both agreed that God had a plan and purpose for her while she was here. She said she didn't plan to be a witness of the Gospel when she came here, but God called her to be one to me in His perfect time.

Regine had to go to some place in Ann Arbor for three days before she flew home. I guess this was a place for her to detach herself emotionally from her stay here in America. Before she left to go there, I went over to her host parents' house to say my final goodbye. We hugged each other while shedding some tears and I realized that **I was saying goodbye to someone who changed my life.** I remember the car pulling out of the driveway of her host parents' house and Regine's face as she waved to me. As the car was out of sight, I took a deep breath and got into my car and drove over to Micah's place. On the drive over to Micah's, I just had this feeling that someone pulled my insides out. I just felt numb, I guess. I didn't realize how much I was connected to Regine until she left.

In my flesh, I was sad to see her go, but in my spirit, I was overwhelmed with being thankful. **I saw clearly that God Almighty in His sovereignty used Regine as the vessel to proclaim Christ Jesus to me. For this reason, she was put into my life – to explain the Good News of Christ crucified.** I realized that she was the one who was obedient to love me unconditionally and not condemn or judge me. And because of her doing that, I was able to hear what she said when she explained Christ crucified. For such a time as then, she was primed to preach the gospel to me and explain the things of God.

Once I realized what God did, it made it easier to know that I would be Ok without her. God used the common ground of music we wrote together as the foundation for us to develop a relationship. Not only the music, but she also made a decision to like the things that I liked doing. Shooting pool or hanging out at the bowling alley was our main thing to do. Sometimes she would come up to the bowling alley and hang out in the cafe and wait for me to get out of work so I could spend time with her and take her home. And of course, there were all of the music rehearsals we had. Not one bad memory of our time together. The time I spent with her led to salvation and healing of my mind, body and soul.

I finally got to Micah's. It was a beautiful sunny day as I made my way around the back of his house to go through the sliding glass doors to get into his pad. I walked in and sat down and hung my head a little. Micah asked me if I was ok. I took a deep breath and sighed and told him that I was ok. I smiled, looked up at him and we joked around for a minute. We tried working on some songs together, but I just was having a hard time staying focused. We both decided that Taco Bell sounded good, so we went out and ate Taco Bell instead. He was a good friend to me and tried to help me transition to life without Regine. After Taco Bell, we went back to his pad to try and work on some music.

Simple Dreams

Around that same time, my band Surreal decided to record CD number two at a recording studio in Owosso, Michigan. It would end up being an EP because we had five songs that the guitar player and vocalist were writing, and I was writing the music on the sixth song. Although the first CD *"Earth Passages of the Illuminated"* was a great CD, these 6 new songs were even better. The vocal arrangements were very engaging, and the music from song to song stood out with its own uniqueness.

Songs like "Child of Glory" and "Of Sea and Sky" really allowed me to write some great bass lines and challenged me to up my game on bass. One big difference between this CD and the first one was the vocals. The vocal arrangements were amazing, and people took note of how good the vocals were on this CD. Over the last 4 years Ben, Scott, and Darius had been singing together and they hit this point of blending well together and sounding as though they were one.

This CD formed a special place in my heart. It contained the first funk/rock song that I wrote, from beginning to end, on my bass guitar. I had some ideas from playing with Craig and Jack, and came up with a cool main riff. Then one day I was having fun jamming with Darius and we started to play this main riff I had and as we kept playing it evolved into this funk rock song. Darius elevated the song to a new level with his drum playing by adding his quick hands to interact with the beat. He used to be a jazz drummer and then Surreal challenged him to be a rock drummer so quick hands were a natural way of playing for him. Darius and I would work on this song before and after Surreal rehearsals until it finally came to completion. I was excited to add it to the second Surreal CD.

I poured my blood, sweat, and tears into that song. I was very proud of what I accomplished on it as a bass player. One of the things that I was able to be proud of, and really display in this song, was my picking technique on the bass. 'Dead notes' really helped make this groove sound great. This was my signature on bass- creating grooves and being funky with a pick on the bass. At the time, I didn't hear any other pick bass players doing what I was doing, so I felt as though I was pioneering something really great on bass.

Another reason I'm proud of this song, is that it is the first song I was able to use a two-hand tapping technique on that was made popular by solo bassists of that time. Two-hand tap was something bass players were trying to do, and I felt as though I was on the cutting edge of this technique. It wasn't anything like a long tap solo. In the middle of the song, each one of us got a 4-beat solo before the guitar solo. This challenged me to step up my game as a tap bass player. My 4-beat solo is where I put the two-hand tapping of an arpeggio. It made me proud because it was something I wrote myself.

The last thing I'm proud of about this song, is that it has a bass/drum solo at the end. Because I played with a pick, I couldn't do the slap bass technique that Les Claypool and Flea were making so popular in the 90's. Instead, I used the syncopated 'dead note' technique to create a groove funk bass solo to end the song. It is what I would consider melodic funk with tons of syncopated dead notes. The whole solo was based on an e minor pentatonic scale and spanned the whole neck range of the bass. This was the icing on the cake.

The band asked me what the song title was, and if I was going to write lyrics for this song. I had no idea what to call the song and there was no way I was going to write lyrics because of the complexity of the music. So, Ben and Scott took on the task of writing the lyrics for this song. They came up with a song title of "Simple Dreams." I thought that was a really cool name for a song. I was curious as to what the lyric and melody sounded like. I didn't hear the lyrics with the melody until we were in the studio. When I did, I was so happy with what they came up with. They admitted that it was a challenge writing lyrics to match this music. But they did and it sounded great. Then to my surprise, Ben and Scott suggested that this song, "Simple Dreams," be the title track to this EP we were recording. I was honored that they would pick my song to be the title track.

The *"Simple Dreams"* CD was released fall of that year, 1992, and it started to open more doors for us to gain attention in the industry. People were responding to it a lot better than the first CD. Within just a few weeks, we were getting air play with the song "Child of Glory" and setting up quality gigs. One gig that we set up was warming up for Rick Emmet, the guitar player/singer in the band Triumph. We also won an award for best new band of the year from Z Rock radio. Now this show was a big deal, not only because we were warming up for Rick Emmet, but Z Rock was going to announce that we won best new band in Detroit at the show. Things seemed to be moving along really well for Surreal.

Calling Me to Trust Him

It was September now and another Michigan fall was in the works. Fall is always a time I reflect and examine my life. I took time to think about the last year of my life- more specifically, from January to September of that year. So much had happened and there was so much transition too. From my band's first ever finished CD being released, to being saved and healed, to writing my first song on guitar with lyric and melody. Then starting my own project while leading other musicians in the studio, and recording another CD with Surreal where my song "Simple Dreams" was the title track. This was a lot to take in and I needed to take a breather to contemplate what was going on in my life.

As I thought about all this, I realized that I could not have done any of this without God Almighty. Only by His mercy and grace did I make it through Surreal's first CD as I dealt with carpal tunnel. Only by His mercy and grace was I saved and healed. There was nothing I could have done to deserve salvation. And because of that salvation and healing, I was able to play my bass and acoustic guitar. And because of being able to do that I was able to write my first song with lyrics and melody. I was also able to play bass on original songs in the studio for my own project and Surreal's second CD.

As I pondered that, I came to realize the impact carpal tunnel would've had on my love for music. At the time of my healing, I was at a point where I was going to give up music because the carpal tunnel was just too painful. I realized that God Almighty turned that around for His Glory. And what an immediate impact I was having on the opportunities God was giving me. My hands felt to be the strongest they had ever been and my technique on bass was at a peak- which was in perfect timing, because these bass lines on my project and Surreal's CD were the best bass lines I wrote to date and the most complicated to execute. I just found that there was nothing I couldn't do on the bass after God Almighty healed me. I was gaining more confidence in the Lord, and I was still amazed and so thankful that He was allowing me to continue with music.

As I would read the Word of God, I would come across Scriptures and songs that helped build up my confidence. Scriptures like *"My son, do not forget my teaching, but let your heart keep my commandments, for length of days and years of life and peace they will add to you. Let not steadfast love and faithfulness forsake you; bind them around your neck; write them on the tablet of your heart. So you will find favor and good success in the sight of God and man. Trust in the Lord with all your heart, and do not lean on your own understanding. In all your ways acknowledge him, and he will make straight your paths. Be not wise in your own eyes; fear the Lord, and turn away from evil. It will be healing to your flesh and refreshment to your bones."* Proverbs 3:1-8 ESV

This Scripture would become a foundation for me in my walk with the Lord. What I was learning was that I was not supposed to put confidence in myself but rather the Lord. Plain and simple, I was supposed to gain confidence in Him and then I will have that assurance I need to step out and accomplish the things the Lord puts in front of me. Take a look at what this Scripture tells us, as children of God, that we are supposed to do: Forget not His teaching, keep His commands, love and be faithful, trust in the Lord, acknowledge Him in all my ways, be not wise in my own eyes, fear the Lord, turn from evil. And after each action, there is a promise that God says will happen: Length of days and peace, find favor with God and man, He will make my paths straight, healing for my body.

I say all this because I realized that I could do nothing within my own strength. I would parallel this with the spiritual strength we need by trusting in the Lord, to the actual regaining of physical strength when the Lord healed me. **I realized that both spiritual and physical came from Him** and I had to continually remind myself of that. Zero confidence within myself, but rather trust the promises of God when I put Him first in my life. This was a valuable lesson the Holy Spirit was showing me. I would pray that I would have the wisdom of His Word and know how to trust in Him.

Writing Lyrics At Work

As I read His Word and prayed at work, I found another wonderful blessing happening. I would bring notepads to work and write down the lyrics that were in my head. I had pocket notepads to make it easy to write it down when they came about. Then I would rewrite them onto a bigger notepad to work on refining them. I would eventually type them out on this computer my dad bought and print them out. After I printed them out, I would make copies so I could give them to others who were working on music with me. But it all started while working my shift at the bowling alley.

A lot of times when I would write the lyrics out on the bigger notepad, I would then take them home and start figuring out the music to put with the lyrics. If I had a melody, it would make it easier to write the music. Because I was afraid to write lyrics and melody at one point in my life, I had a lot of guitar and bass riffs in my back pocket. When I would write these riffs, I would have the mindset that someday I'd be able to use them for something. I would get home after work, which would sometimes be as late as 1:00 AM, and sit at my parent's piano in the living room to mess around with chords and progressions. Then I would pick up my acoustic guitar and start playing some of the riffs I wrote to see if anything caught my ear to fit a lyric that I just wrote. Most of the time I wouldn't be able to match a riff to a lyric. But I would always try and see if I could get something to work.

This process of songwriting made sense to me. Some people I knew would just be able to sit down and write a song within a half hour. Not me. I would write and then rewrite and worry over each song that it may not be right. Then I would arrange and rearrange and change parts out. And most of the time I would get back to the original idea with the first riff that caught my ear.

It's like I have to exhaust every possibility in my brain to feel good about the direction of the song. If there is no direction, then I won't give up on the possibilities. This can be very exhausting, and I found myself being worn out from writing music. Every song that I wrote had all of my full attention and I always felt like I would invest all of myself into each song. It was like a relationship. I couldn't stop thinking about the music and lyrics that were pouring out of me. You could say that music had once again become my first love.

Desiring My Own Band

As I was trying to write songs, it was around this time that I started to entertain the idea of starting my own band. I just got done doing something with Regine and Micah along with some guest musicians. But I knew that would be a short-lived experience with Regine having to go back home. I thought maybe we could make it work but it wasn't realistic. As I thought about it some more, I realized that I wanted to step out and form my own band. I just didn't know if it was something I should do. I loved being in Surreal and I wanted to see the band go places and it seemed like we were in a good position to make a run at getting signed by a record label. Something was in my gut that I had to leave the band.

I was working my job, writing new music, and struggling with what to do about staying in Surreal or starting my own band. It was the typical conversation I would have with myself like in the past. One side saying I'm not good enough to start a band and lead on my own, and the other encouraging me to step up and be a leader. It was not hard to be a leader with Regine and Micah because I knew them. Now, I would have to find new band members. People who I would have to get to know. There was a lot swirling up in my brain during this time.

Things are moving along with Surreal, and we seem to be finding favor with the local scene in Detroit. More gigs were in the works, and it seemed like we were on our way. Then, for some reason, we started to have more disagreements between each other. And it was getting more intense as we came closer to Christmas of that year. We ended up doing the concert, opening up for Rick Emmett, and it went well. We received much praise as a band. But it was becoming more and more clear to me that I had to move on from Surreal. After the concert we decided to keep rehearsing even though our next gig was a way out in March, warming up for 38 Special. I've been in the trenches with these guys for about 4 years practicing, recording and gigging. I really didn't want to disappoint them and let them down.

I finally got up the courage to talk to them at one of the

rehearsals and let them know that I was moving on. I don't know if it was a surprise to them or not. I told them I was going to start my own band and record the music that I was working on. I reassured them that I would stay through the 38 Special show. I told them I would even help the next bass player they brought in to replace me learn my bass lines.

I was having a moment during this rehearsal when we took a break from rehearsing and there was this audible voice that came to my head, and it said to me "You will be nothing without me. You cannot do this without me." Wherever the voice came from I don't know but one thing I did know is that it was not of God. But this voice seemed so real, and it really affected me at that moment. My stomach sank and all I could do was sit there and be silent. I started to doubt myself that maybe this voice is right. Maybe I should reconsider my resignation from the band. But something told me to just stick to my decision and not be moved by what anyone else says. I stuck to my decision to resign. When I left rehearsal that night I felt as though a burden was lifted and I felt in my spirit that everything was going to be ok.

38 Special

While my new band is starting to gel together, I was still going to Surreal rehearsals for the 38 Special concert. It was a different culture within the band for sure. I still felt as though I let them down, but to my surprise, the atmosphere was light and seemed relaxed between us. This was a relief for me because I don't like to make people upset with me. I remember Scott even taking interest as to how my new band was doing. I thought that was very cool.

The day of the 38 Special show arrives, and I remember loading up my dad's suburban to head down to Detroit. I was super excited to do this show. I'm always excited to gig out, but this one had an extra special vibe about it. As I got down there and began to unload my equipment, I remember there was just a sense of expectation like it was going to be an awesome show. Everyone was just relaxed and in a good mood.

Darius got his drums set up and we were ready to go for a sound check. Everything went really smooth, and the sound guy dialed in a perfect stage mix. Then 38 Special goes up there to do their sound check. They sounded great as usual. I remember one of their sound guys spraying Lysol on all the microphones. I thought that was odd but then it made sense to kill the germs and anything else from other singers using the mic. The sound checks were done, and the stage was set and ready to go.

It was almost time for us to go on and I remember the feeling was electrifying for me. As I looked out to see how many people were in the crowd, to my surprise it was almost a full house! I got this nervous feeling in my gut, and I had to get my mind ready to do this show. A lot of emotion was swirling in my head. This was the last show with Surreal at my favorite place to play and it was the biggest crowd I've ever played in front of. I was told Harpos sold around 5000 tickets for that night. There were at least 3500 people already there when we went on. I thought to myself that tonight was going to be awesome.

The lights come on and we go out to start our show. The crowd starts to get louder and louder and we start our first song- "Child of Glory." When we were done with that song the crowd reaction is something I'll never forget. They were loud and responded with affirmation that they liked the song. It was the beginning of an amazing night. With each song the interaction with the crowd became more intense. This was something I never experienced until that night. I remember being on my side of the stage just taking in the best performance we did as a band. We were tight and the vocals were spot on the whole set and the crowd loved every minute of what we did. We hit the ending of the set and and did the typical rock ending of everyone jamming on a certain chord until the very end and then we hit the last chord. The crowd went nuts. I remember that feeling like it was yesterday. What a perfect ending to a part of my life I am so grateful for.

Contemplation

One day, while I was having coffee, I was pondering this idea of how the Holy Spirit orchestrates the events in my life. I started to think about how the year of 1992 was a mass symphony of transitions in my life. I am convinced that the Holy Spirit was making everything happen. Everyone that the Holy Spirit used was not saved or a Christian, but every person was used for what God wanted to see happen in my life. Almost like there was a designed plan or something and somehow all these people were used by the Lord for His purpose. I heard the Pastor say to me, "God has a plan and a purpose for your life." I would always nod my head as if I knew what he was talking about, but in all reality I didn't. It was a concept that boggled my mind. In the past, I saw people in the right place at the right time as being a coincidence, not God's plan and purpose. Now I had to rethink the idea of coincidence and subscribe to the idea that God does have a plan and a purpose for everyone. This was something new for me to think about and try to understand.

Around this same time of pondering the idea that God has a plan and purpose for everyone, I come across this verse in the Word of God: *"The Lord will fulfill his purpose for me; your steadfast love, O Lord, endures forever. Do not forsake the work of your hands."* Psalm 138:8 ESV. This was one of those verses that jumped off the page. I read it again, and then again. What stuck out to me was the Lord will fulfill His purpose for me. I asked myself how the Lord would fulfill His purpose for me and what that will look like. I asked myself what does it even mean to have purpose? I wasn't so sure. It seemed so out of reach for me and like it was some sort of alien concept. I started to pray about this idea of purpose.

When I was done praying, I couldn't help but to think about how planning and purpose work together. I thought about whether they are the same thing or not. It didn't make sense that they were the same thing. Planning seemed to be about action. You put a plan into action by following a step-by-step procedure. That was my thinking anyway. Then I thought about whether God had a step-by-step procedure for my life. What were the steps I would follow to walk out God's plan and purpose for my life? Maybe I was already following His plan for me, and I didn't even realize it.

For some reason it started to make sense that I was in God's plan all along. I just was not the one putting the plan into action and had nothing to do with the plan or the outcome. Regine was the one to preach the gospel to me, and salvation and healing was not something I planned, it just happened. The first song with lyrics and melody was not something I planned, it just happened. The music I recorded with Regine and Surreal was something I planned though…right? No, it was not. God gave me the talent to play bass and then healed me of what was trying to destroy that talent. I didn't plan that at all. And now I'm venturing off to start my own band and record my own CD. That had to be my plan. Nope! As I thought about it, I realized that it was the Holy Spirit guiding me in all this and there every step of the way. It was He who put in my spirit to step out and be a leader even though I had no idea what was going to happen.

I had to trust the Lord and believe that He was with me every step of the way. To put my confidence in Him and not try and forcefully figure things out. I rested well that night after that time I had with the Lord drinking a coffee pondering these things. I didn't need to know the plan, I just had to follow the plan as it unfolds. I made a decision that night before bed that I would follow the Lord's leading for my life.

CHAPTER 5
"Something New"

"And the Lord answered me: "Write the vision; make it plain on tablets, so he may run who reads it." Habakkuk 2:2 ESV

New Chapter

Soon after I left Surreal, I had some time for good contemplation. I felt as though another chapter of my life was closed and a new blank page was put in front of me. Like I would start to write a new chapter in my life from that day forward. I have to admit, I didn't know what to expect to happen, but I had a sense of expectation and excitement. I really had no back up plan and no one who could mentor me to know how to start my own band. I knew that I had to find band members and record the music. There had to be more to it than that. I mean I can always find musicians it seems like, and I've already done studio recording. These were not foreign concepts to me.

Of course, being a guy who makes lists all the time, I already made all kinds of lists for this journey of starting my own band. Lists like what songs to record, the places we could play, what kind of band I wanted, equipment we were going to need to play live. I also printed out the lyrics of the songs I had so they would be ready to give to new band members. This was the easy stuff to do as the leader. Lots of thinking and paperwork.

One thing I learned is that I had to display a sense of confidence as band members joined. No one wants to join a group if the leadership is unsure of themselves. I had to figure out quickly how to project confidence and give the new members a sense that this band will be worth their time. I knew this from experience with two other bands I was in before this one. My high school band was always a joy to go to and write music with, and the band Surreal was well-organized, had structure, and direction. I always knew what was going on and why. I wouldn't want to waste my time with a band that has no direction. Because they projected direction, I was able to show up to rehearsals with confidence that this band was worth my time. I asked myself the question: How do I create a sense of direction for this band I'm starting? This is something I would have to think about and ponder.

    I was on the second shift, so I would often go out on my parents' deck in the late morning/early afternoon to think about things. The next day while I was there having coffee, the word 'vision' came to mind. The word 'vision' continued to pop up in my spirit as I drank my coffee. I thought to myself what does vision even mean? What is it? I started to think maybe vision has something to do with having direction. As I thought about that, I started to realize that maybe I needed vision for this undertaking of starting a band.

    It came to my mind that I needed to think about vision from a business standpoint. I remembered Micah telling me that you cast vision to see your goals through to completion. For example, running a business. That made sense to me. All big and small businesses have a vision as to what they want to accomplish. Some people claim to have visions of the future, and others refer to vision in the physical eye sense. I needed to understand vision from a business sense.

    The next day I looked up the definition of vision. It simply said that it is *aspiring to where I want to go*. That made sense to me as I thought about it. Then I thought about where I wanted to go with this new adventure of starting a band. The one thing I wanted was to be signed by a major label. I concluded that the vision for this band was to be signed by a major label. According to the definition of vision it made sense to say that being signed by a major label is where I wanted to be. Therefore, that would be our vision.

Understanding the end goal of being signed by a major label gave me a sense of direction. Because of this vision I believed that I could invest my time and resources into getting signed. I started to get focused, and I now had a target to shoot for. This was an amazing revelation for me. This verse in the Scriptures took on a whole new meaning *"Trust in the Lord with all your heart, and do not lean on your own understanding. In all your ways acknowledge him, and he will make straight your paths."* Proverbs 3:5-6 ESV. With this new direction on my heart to be signed by a major label, I knew that I needed to trust the Lord and let Him direct my path. I continued to pray for wisdom with this new adventure and continued to acknowledge Him in all my ways.

Finding Band Mates

I was already talking to Micah about starting my own band before I resigned from Surreal. He offered to be the lead singer of my new band. That was a good start. He knew a guitar player who was just getting out of high school too. I was a little skeptical at first, but we auditioned him. When I heard him play his guitar, I couldn't believe how mature his playing was. We invited him to join the band. Now I needed a keyboard player and drummer. The new guitar player's best friend was a keyboard player. After auditioning him and talking with him, we invited him to join the band. All I needed was a drummer. I remember a guy I went to school with who was a drummer. I ran into him a few months back at a pawn shop he worked at in Flint, MI. I thought to myself- Why not go and pay him a visit? I went up to this pawn shop and sure enough, he was still working there. I got to talking with him and after a few visits he ended up joining the band as well. Now, I had my first band lined up.

Now, with each new band member, I had to explain what

the vision was for the band. Simply put, I wanted the band to be signed by a major label. They all acknowledged that and said they were cool with learning originals to record in the studio and pursue this vision with me. I found casting vision to those in the band from the start laid down expectations. My hope was everyone would buy into this vision and put their best foot forward to make it happen. So far, so good.

I had to do my part as the leader and give us direction as to what we should start to do. I wanted to start with working on original music of songs that I wrote. Even though there was talk of doing cover songs among the other band members, I was more interested in starting out working original music. Besides, doing cover songs did not line up with the vision of this band. Bringing that to remembrance, I made cassettes of my bass lines for each song and gave it to the band members. I simply asked them to listen to the song and come back to the next rehearsal prepared to work on the songs so we can get them down.

The first song I wanted everyone to work on was a song I wrote called "Can You Feel the Power." It was a heavy metal song with some tasty tempo changes. The next rehearsal, the band members showed up and had parts together so we could start working on arranging it. The band was doing a great job getting it down. It would seem that things were moving along well, so we decided that we were ready to take on another original the following week. This would go on for a while and we were building confidence as a band.

Division Starts

Then one day the drummer asked when we were going to start working on cover songs so we could go out and play the bars. When he asked this, I really didn't want the conflict. So, I basically told him we would start after we learned the original songs. Which at that time we only had one more to learn. I wasn't against learning cover songs because they would get us some gigs to allow us to play the originals within the set. But I didn't want to focus on covers until the originals were down. This conversation of wanting to do cover songs started to cast division in the band. Because the drummer would not let up on wanting to do cover songs, the guitar player and the key player started to take sides with the drummer and gang up on me during rehearsals. It was a new challenge for me.

Before one rehearsal the other band members talked amongst themselves until I got there. Then all three were on one side of the room and I was on the other side. Almost like we were in a fight match or something and when we started to talk about what we would do for rehearsal that night- it was like a bell went off to start a fight. This was not what I expected from them. After all, we all agreed to the vision of getting a record deal and being signed. They started to threaten me by saying that they would leave the band if we didn't start learning cover songs. This created a problem and I had to figure out what to do so they wouldn't leave the band. This would be the first time dealing with strife among band members and would be the first challenge as a leader for me to deal with and overcome.

I was able to weather that confrontation for now, and when rehearsal was done that night, I was able to take it to the Lord in prayer. I just felt like I could not back down and had to hold my ground by saying we are going to do original songs like we agreed in the beginning. I couldn't change the direction of the vision. This frustrated the drummer, guitar and key player. It was obvious their attitude changed, and they were becoming difficult to handle. I keep thinking as the leader I would have to learn to resolve conflict and manage everyone's feelings.

Before the next rehearsal, the guitar player announced that he was going to Seattle to pursue his dreams of being a grunge guitar player. He was such an incredible grunge and blues player, and let me tell you, he had the chops to back it. Not only did I miss his talent, but he was a funny storyteller. The most memorable story he told was about the three-legged chicken. It was hilarious the way he told it.

There was this instrumental song I wrote that he really liked to play with me. I was struggling to find a name for the song, so he said the song reminded him of the story of the three-legged chicken. Every time he said that story everyone in the band would be on the floor laughing. We jokingly added the phrase 'the legend' in front of the title of the 'three-legged chicken'. We thought that the song should be titled "The Legend of the Three-Legged Chicken". Later on, down the road I shortened it to "The Legend".

After the guitar player left for Seattle, Micah knew of another guitar player who would be a good fit, Sam. We talked to him about our vision as a band and how we wanted to record originals and get signed. He agreed to join the band knowing what we were wanting to accomplish. Just as I started to teach Sam the originals the drummer had a meltdown. He started to go off on all of us one night and kicked all of us out of his basement and dismantled the band. This was very disheartening. I was crushed. What was I supposed to do now? I just quit my band Surreal not too long ago to pursue my dream of having my own band. Then just as we were getting the original songs together, we had a breakup. It was very deflating. The keyboard player decided to move on and not wait around to find another drummer. Both Micah and Sam decided to stick around to see this vision through.

I had a moment with the Lord on my way home that night and I just didn't know what to do so I prayed. I questioned God as to whether I was actually hearing His voice in this whole thing. If the Holy Spirit was leading, then why am I looking for more band members. Did I miss it the first time with those band members? Was I supposed to work on cover songs and play bars? I was frustrated and needed to vent to the Lord. So, I did. Then the three of us started to brainstorm people we would bring into the band. I prayed and asked God for direction as to what to do.

New Drummer

The next day I felt on my heart to call my old drummer from Surreal, Darius. Funny story how Darius and I became band mates in Surreal. Surreal went through band member replacements as well, and there came a time when we needed a new drummer. Ben had a job at the Sheraton hotel in Flint, Michigan, and he worked the night shift. Because of this, he was able to watch the music performers that the hotel was bringing in for their dinner entertainment. There was this father/son duo that was booked there for about 2 months, and Ben became friends with the drummer of this duo.

One day Ben called me in the afternoon to tell me this drummer was interested in joining Surreal and that his talent was off the chain. He asked me to bring my bass and amp up to the hotel to meet this drummer after they were done with their music set.

I said, "You want me to be there at what time?"
He said, "1 AM".
I responded, "Dude..for real?"
I have to admit I was not enthusiastic about doing this, but Ben went on about how good this drummer was and how he would be a good fit for our band.

I went up to the Sheraton hotel at 1 AM, dragged my equipment into where they are set up to meet this drummer. I didn't know what to expect when I went up there. Ben got my attention and brought me over to meet Darius. At first, I was like "whaaaat" and had to chuckle. Here was this big, black dude, probably 275, fit and dressed in some sort of alien-like outfit with noticeable makeup on his face, a whole tube of gel in his hair and glitter all over his head, arms and outfit. I thought to myself "What the heck am I doing here at 1AM to jam with this dude?"

Ben introduced us, and we shook hands and made some small talk for a minute. He told me that he was from Jersey and he and his dad were a touring duo of which his dad played the keyboard, and both did vocals. Then when I met his Dad, it made sense why Darius was dressed the way he was. His dad had the same type of outfit with glitter in his hair and on his face. It was all a part of their act. I was like "ahh I get it now." Darius said he'd be right back as the dinner area was clearing out. About 20 minutes later he came back out in street clothes ready to jam. He sat down on his kit and was messing around, getting loose to jam with me and I have to say I started to get a little excited. Just from what I heard of him messing around was really good.

I started to play a funky impromptu riff and Darius nodded his head twice and came in with an amazing drum beat. He locked in with me right away with no struggle to find the pocket. There was no pushing or pulling against each other at all. It was like I've been jamming with the dude for a long time, we just clicked. Everything each one of us played, the other was right there in sync. We played funky riffs and driving riffs and everything in between. This was the beginning of a wonderful drum/bass relationship.

Darius and I went through so much together in Surreal and were so familiar with each other, I was really hoping he would join my new band. When I called Darius to ask if he wanted to join my band, he didn't have to think very hard about it and gave me a confident 'Yes.' We made small talk about the direction of the band and what my end goal was, which was to get signed. This was a huge lift that I needed. Knowing that Darius was on board breathed life back into pursuing this vision. I took tapes of the songs over to his house so he could listen to them before the next rehearsal.

New Line Up

As word spread that I needed band members through friends I was able to connect with a guitar player, Tom King and a keyboard player, Mark Siefert. I knew Tom from Micah. They went to school together, and Tom was an upcoming guitar player in the area who just happened to be available. Mark was a friend of a friend, and he always wanted to be in a rock band. I was happy to bring them on board with this band. They both seemed excited to join up with me and write original music, with the end goal of getting signed. We were now a full band again. Every single one of us in the band wanted to do originals as the main focus. We were all on the same page.

Soon after the new band line up starts to rehearse, Micah approached me to tell me that he is having problems with his throat. This was causing issues with his singing voice. He was having a hard time retaining control of notes and his range was affected as well. He told me that he needed surgery. After he said that, he decided it would be best that he stepped down as the vocalist and exit the band. I know this was hard on him because he wanted to make music his life and his voice was his instrument. After his surgery, his voice never seemed to be the same. My heart broke for him because I could relate to what it is like to have your instrument taken away due to a physical issue. We stayed friends and supported each other after that.

Now I needed to find a vocalist. Tom suggested that we run an ad looking for a prog rock vocalist. I had no idea how to do that but thank goodness Tom knew how. Within a few days we had several responses and started to set up auditions. Out of all the auditions, there were few who were good. But there was one vocalist who was amazing and stuck out to me, Chris Lopez. I liked him from the moment he showed up to the audition, and was hoping he would have the vocals we needed. He started singing the song we gave him. I couldn't believe what I heard! It was the Ronnie James Dio/ Bruce Dickinson voice I wanted. His voice was a perfect fit, and I had a peace in my spirit about him. We brought him into the band right away. After Chris joined the band, we were ready to roll and get this band back on track.

One of the things that we had to do was change our band name. We unofficially named the band Euphorix. That name was not resonating with me or the rest of the band anymore. We started kicking around some band names. One idea was Scrypture, purposely misspelled. That name didn't work. Then the name Liquid Eclipse came to mind. I thought about this name and wondered if I should make this the band name. Liquid Eclipse was the name of a piece of music I wrote in Surreal. I wondered if that would be too weird to name the band after a bass composition I wrote. I just couldn't get the name Liquid Eclipse out of my head, so I presented that name to the other members. They all thought it was a good name for the band. It sounded like a name for a prog rock band. We rolled with it.

As this new band with a new line up started to get together, there was a sense of community and acceptance among us. Tom was more business-like and kept us focused on planning and setting goals. Mark was a nerd who was sarcastic at times, and led a youth group at church as his occupation, but added an awesome dynamic with his piano playing and pads from his Roland gear. Sam was just a trooper driving a long way to get to practice and was committed to the vision. Chris was someone who made us all laugh and kept things light as we rehearsed and wrote music. Darius was the quiet type who always challenged us to think bigger and come prepared. All of us were talented but more importantly we all brought something to help bring a sense of fellowship and community to the band. We all supported each other and made each other laugh. And this would set the tone for what was to come as a band.

Demo

We spent a lot of time practicing in Darius's basement getting these original songs together for our demo. This was a huge leap for us to move the band forward, because it was holding us accountable to know our parts and come prepared. During this time, I also found out that Darius, Mark, and Tom could sing really good harmonies well together. This was an unexpected dynamic I didn't plan on. But I was so happy that they were doing this because it elevated the songs we were writing. They would spend time just practicing the harmonies to the instrument tracks that we already laid down for our demo.

When the demo was complete, it opened up doors for us as a band to play out. We ended up playing at Contos in Flint, Michigan quite a bit after this demo. We also played at a place called the I-Rock near Detroit. There was one gig we did in Stanton, MI on Labor Day weekend at a battle of the bands contest. We ended up getting an afternoon spot which is not a prime time to play. But because we went out there and didn't complain and put on a stellar show the event coordinator promised us a prime spot the following year. This was good for the band because it would tighten us up musically and vocally.

We kept writing songs and working at making them gig-ready. And after some months, we decided it was time to start recording these songs in the studio. We talked about what studio to use, from The Disc in Detroit to a popular studio in Owosso, MI. It made sense to me to goto the recording studio in Owosso. We agreed that the quality of this studio was great, based on the Surreal CD "Simple Dreams," which of course I was a part of. And this studio was affordable for the band. I called the owner and set the date to start recording the bed-tracks.

A Deck Moment

Taking a moment out on my parent's deck with a cup of coffee, I was reflecting on Liquid Eclipse and what we were doing. As I thought about it, I realized that God was there every step of the way. He brought this band line up together and the Holy Spirit put on my heart the band name. It was like everything was falling into place and all the details were covered. Then the Holy Spirit impressed on my heart of being a part of a possible ministry that was music-related. I really didn't understand it at the time because Liquid Eclipse was not a Christian band. I wasn't even too sure what the other band members believed. Except for Mark, because he was a Youth Pastor. I would ponder these things in my heart and keep them to myself for now.

As I sat on my deck drinking tea, it dawned on me that this was a time in my life when I was able to apply the idea of keeping the vision in front of me. Vision was a foreign concept to me until the Lord started to show me how *vision is the foundation of accomplishing anything specific*. With vision, I can always see the end goal of where I want to be. Vision also brought clarity as to what decisions needed to be made while I moved towards that end goal.

I found that vision made it easy to make tough decisions. If opportunities arose that would take me away from where I wanted to be, then I would have to decline the offer. In my band, if it didn't line up with the vision, then we as a band would not do it. To be signed by a major label you cannot get away from doing original songs. When the first band members were buffeting against the vision, it made it easy to stand my ground.

Since I was a young boy, I wanted to tour the world and be signed by a major label. It was a dream of mine for was long as I can remember. I always enjoyed live music and the atmosphere that goes along with it. Desiring to be signed to go on the road was a no brainer for me. With all this revelation of vision, I knew that I should write it down. I found some paper and I wrote two words... Get Signed. That was it. God Almighty in His Word said that we are supposed to write the vision down *"And the Lord answered me: "Write the vision; make it plain on tablets, so he may run who reads it."* Habakkuk 2:2 ESV

I learned that it is very easy to get knocked off course of the vision that was put in my heart. I needed this time with the Lord Almighty to regain confidence in what He put in my heart. I wasn't going to be moved by anyone's opinion of what they think I should be doing. **Stay the course, stay focused, stay strong and let God make the vision come to pass.**

CHAPTER 6
"Only Love Remains"

"But you are a chosen race, a royal priesthood, a holy nation, a people for his own possession, that you may proclaim the excellencies of him who called you out of darkness into his marvelous light. Once you were not a people, but now you are God's people; once you had not received mercy, but now you have received mercy."
1 Peter 2:9-10 ESV

We Should Have Purpose

As we were preparing for the studio, I wanted to rethink the vision of this band along with our plan and purpose. I already knew the vision I had for the band: Get Signed. I was also aware of the plan, which was to write songs, rehearse songs, perform songs, and record songs. If we wanted to get signed and acquire meaningful gigs, we would have to have a product to sell- that being a CD. I saw this clearly as we were moving forward as a band.

But I was struggling to be able to tell anyone the purpose for the band. The *'why'* do we exist as a band. For whatever reason, nothing came to mind as to the purpose of Liquid Eclipse. Someone out of the blue asked me if I knew the purpose of my band and I couldn't answer them. It was definitely an eye opener for me at the time. I couldn't figure out why it bothered me so much though. I mean, we had direction as to where we wanted to go, so why did I need to know the purpose of the band? Isn't knowing the vision and plan enough? I thought to myself,

I'll tuck this thought away for the time being and maybe revisit it down the road.

Only Love Remains

There was a lot going on in the battlefield of my mind. I started thinking about the battle of good and evil that rages around me. How God pursued me and pulled me out of the miry clay of my sin and set my feet upon the rock. I also thought about how the devil also pursues me to make my life miserable or even deceive me into rejecting God. This would cause me to think about whether or not I could lose my salvation. Some Christians I talked to would tell me that I could not be plucked out of the hand of God. Which would mean that the devil could not cause me to lose my salvation. Others would tell me I could lose my salvation at the drop of a hat. If I had any unrepented sin for the day, then I lost it. Almost like if I sinned once I would go to hell. This was very confusing to me. If I could end up in hell because I sinned, then who could be saved? I thought to myself after all, we are going to sin. We cannot stop ourselves from sinning.

I knew I was saved, but I was still wrestling with this idea of my eternal salvation and sin. I saw this as a battle over the souls of God's creation. The devil pursues me because he thinks that I am rightfully his, because by nature I am sinful. But God's love has crushed the power of sin and destroyed the works of the devil. I knew according to the Word of God that I am His and I was bought at a price. *"Or do you not know that your body is a temple of the Holy Spirit within you, whom you have from God? You are not your own, for you were bought with a price. So glorify God in your body."* 1 Corinthians 6:19-20 ESV. I also saw in Scriptures, nothing could snatch me from the hand of God *"I give them eternal life, and they will never perish, and no one will snatch them out of my hand. My Father, who has given them to me, is greater than all, and no one is able to snatch them out of the Father's hand. I and the Father are one.""* John 10:28-30 ESV. The devil in his arrogance will still seek to destroy my life. I knew I had found hope, and the love of God was amazing. It was, and still is, something I can't fully understand. With this in mind, I started to write a new song. These are the words that came out of me at this time.

The eyes of time seek your way, what did you see
A path of hell looking for you, as time goes on and on
What has come of me, give me something to hang to
All I need is you, oh yes you
The eyes of time seek my way, what did I see
A path of hell looking for me, as time went on and on

As these words resonated with me, the song needed a chorus. The guitar player Tom was always inviting me over to write music together outside of rehearsals. After talking to Tom about these words I wrote, he invited me over to his house so we could work together and come up with a chorus. I went over there, and we spent the evening kicking ideas around. Eventually, we hit on something and wrote this incredible anthem chorus. When we finally agreed to the lyrics and music of the chorus, we really believed we came up with something special.

The chorus in its simplicity captured the idea of where I was once deceived and in the painful darkness, and now that I am in His kingdom after He came and found me. I will remain in His love. This was a Selah moment for me. Almost like an epiphany. This night was a turning point for the band. What was written for this chorus perfectly completed the song. We titled the song "Only Love Remains."

I have seen the darkness, And I have felt the pain
But now that I have found You, Only Love Remains

I took what Tom, and I wrote that night along with the words I wrote and worked really hard at arranging the song. I finally came up with something I liked. The next step was to start showing Darius this arrangement. I ended up working with Darius a few times before rehearsals to see if the arrangement sounded good. Mind you, I would do this with my acoustic guitar. I really wanted to get this song on the project we were working on. I mentioned adding this song to the list of songs we were going to record in the studio. I really didn't push for the rest of the band to work on this song until Darius and I had it together. Darius figured we would save it for a future project. I thought about that and had to agree that the song wasn't quite ready for this project. After all, the studio date was fast approaching.

Studio Weekend

The studio weekend arrives, and we are excited. We booked two days to record all the bed tracks for these songs that we wrote and arraigned. We have two twelve-hour days to get the bed-tracks done and to tape. The studio was up five flights of stairs. I couldn't believe all the stuff we had to take up those stairs to set up. Especially Darius's drums- his drum set was huge! The guitar players had half stacks and many guitars as well. All I had was a preamp and one bass. But we all helped each other out and got set up in no time. Good times!

As we started recording, I had a sense of peace and was just so happy. I felt as though the vision was making so many strides with this band. The only nerve-racking thing of the whole weekend was deciding if what we just recorded was good enough. When we started doing the recording, we ended up only needing a few run throughs for each song. We didn't have the luxury of unlimited hours of studio time and reels of tape, so it was great that we were getting it down in a few takes. I had it planned out so we would only need 3 reels of tape. I also had to plan the order of recording the songs so we could fit all the songs on the three reels of tape. Everything was going as planned. The band was tight, and the sound of the drums and bass were coming out great.

We just got done tracking the last song of the two days and we had some time left over. Everyone went home except for Darius and me. He thought we were done, and he was getting ready to be on his way home. The Holy Spirit was telling me to record "Only Love Remains" even though we decided to not record it for this project. I was a little stressed about this and hesitant to ask Darius to stay. But the Holy Spirit kept pressing into my heart to record this song with Darius, right then, and there. I asked Darius if he could stay and lay down the drum tracks for this song really quick before he went home. I could tell he was upset, and after an intense moment of fellowship with him, he decided to do it.

I grabbed my acoustic guitar and got ready to record this song. The engineer of the studio set me up to record this guitar part with the drums. While he was doing that, I was talking the arrangement through with Darius to remind him how it went. I wanted to be right there next to Darius so he could see my cues.

Darius looked at me before we hit the record button and said, "I will only run through this song one time then I have to go".

Not sure what was going on with him that night, but the Holy Spirit kept him there to record this song.

The engineer was ready. He hit the record button, and I started playing the acoustic guitar in the beginning and away we went. I don't know who played those drums and guitar when the engineer hit the record button, but we went through this song from beginning to end and did not miss a beat, a change, or anything. It was like God's holy angels were right there making sure this song was recorded. When we were done with our one time run through, I had such a peace come over me. I couldn't stop smiling and I felt as though this made the CD complete. The drum part Darius played was awesome!

This song, "Only Love Remains," ended up being a band collaboration after the bed-tracks were done. Chris Lopez's vocals were strong and unbelievable. His presentation was spot on. I couldn't sing at the time, so the band wrote and put together all the background vocals for this song and actually the whole album. Darius had these high soaring backup vocals and Mark and Tom sounded great as well with tenor and baritone parts. Mark took the bed tracks home that Darius and I recorded and wrote an amazing piano part for the song and middle string section. I'll never forget the first time I heard the piano part Mark wrote. It was amazingly perfect and moving, which created the direction for the song.

Record Label Seminar

There was an amazing opportunity that came to Flint, Michigan while we were recording the Liquid Eclipse CD in the studio. Major record labels from everywhere were putting on a weekend seminar for bands, artists, and producers to help them understand how to go about being signed by a major label. Atlantic records, EMI records, Capitol records and other major labels were present at this weekend event. This really fired the band up and we became super excited. This was something that doesn't happen ever in the Flint area. With excitement, we paid the money and got our tickets to attend.

We became even more excited when we found out at the end of the last day of the seminar the record labels would do a Q and A with anyone who wanted to attend. To top it off they were allowing bands to submit one song for them to listen to and then they would give their feedback on the song and give you tips on how to make it better. We ended up picking the song "What Has Come of Me" from our songs in the studio. It just happens to have all the parts recorded and was a good song to submit. We did a quick mix of the song and brought it with us.

It's our turn for us to play our song for the record labels to critique. After they listened to it, they actually had good things to say about it and gave us some good tips to make it a better song. At the end of this weekend, we were able to hand each record label a copy of our song, bio, and pictures. It was an amazing experience for us as a band, and really motivated us to continue to push through and keep going. It can be very draining when trying to put together everything to present to record labels. And the rejection can be hard to take as well. But it was nice to get positive feedback on our song, which helped us gain confidence about our direction.

Stanton

There was a battle of the bands on Labor Day weekend in Stanton, Michigan of that year, 1995. I played there a couple years before with a different band and so I thought it would be a great opportunity to get out and perform. This would end up being our 2nd year in a row as Liquid Eclipse competing in this battle of the bands. The first year we didn't get a good time slot, so we didn't get much response from the crowd that was there. The coordinator of the contest noted that we were pretty good and promised that we would get a good time slot this time around. He followed through with his promise and we received a prime-time slot- 7pm on Saturday night.

We got up to Stanton, found a spot to park, and started to mingle with the bands as we waited for our turn to perform. This place was a campground/motocross racing track that had a big grass area with an outdoor stage for all the bands to play. I think there were 30 bands that weekend to compete in this battle of the bands. This place was like a big weekend party. Although nobody in the band partied, we still wanted to have a great show. I have to admit I was a little nervous being there, but I believed we were supposed to be there.

As it was getting closer for us to go on and play, we noticed the crowd diminishing more and more after each band before us. This was quite alarming I have to say. Then the band right before us starts in with their song set. Now, I like to listen to some good heavy metal just like the next guy, but these guys were horrible.

It was like nothing I ever heard or experienced. The music wasn't the problem. It was the lyrical content. The message that their songs said was blasphemous towards God Almighty. It was Satanic at the very least. And now the crowd was down to almost nobody.

Mark, who was like the spiritual leader of the band, was the one who noticed that the crowd was depleted. He also was the one who pointed out that the lyrical content was blasphemous. Something ignited a fire under Mark when he realized that, and he became righteously angry. As him and I talked, we agreed that we should pray. I was going to go pray quietly on my own, but Mark insisted we pray together as a band. I was really hesitant to do that but as the leader of the band, I gathered all of us together and Mark led us in prayer. I don't remember exactly what he prayed, but I do remember it was a prayer of spiritual warfare. He used phrases like 'pull down the stronghold' and 'cast out the enemy'. He also asked God to bring back the people to hear His word through the music and lyrics He gave Liquid Eclipse. I felt in my spirit after we were done praying there was a battle that had been won and the door was open to share the Good News of Jesus from the stage.

That band was finally done, and it was our turn to hit the stage. I had a conversation with the singer Chris before we went on and I asked him if he felt comfortable proclaiming Christ and Glorifying His Name tonight on stage. He said no problem, which I was happy to hear. I knew Chris had a Christian background, but I wasn't sure if he would step out to evangelize. I'm continuing to pray in my heart as we are setting up and getting ready. I had to do this so I could empty myself and give it to God Almighty. There was every chance to have a negative attitude and complain. This was a moment where I was continuing to trust God and believe that He hears and answers prayer.

We started playing our first song with no one in the crowd. Then, slowly but surely, people started making their way out from their campsites to come listen to us. Mark looked over to me and smiled, as if to say God is answering prayer. I felt the power of the Holy Spirit over me right then as we continued to play. By the time we were done with our set there were many people who were watching and listening to Liquid Eclipse perform. Glory to God! After we were done, there were so many people complimenting us and wanting to hear more. Even the event coordinator commented on how we were better than the year before and how amazed he was at the people coming back from their campsites to watch us. He said he had never seen that happen before.

Setting aside all the compliments, the most important thing that happened was the Gospel went forth that night and God the Father was glorified. The Presence of God fell on us on the stage and the people who watched us that night. As people were complimenting us on our music, there were others who were asking more about who Jesus was and questions of the Bible. The Holy Spirit gave us ample opportunity to proclaim Christ crucified. To God be the Glory!! We did not claim to be a Christian band, but the Holy Spirit was still working through us and the message of the lyrics.

As I was winding down from the excitement of preaching the gospel after our show, a young lady told me she could not stop crying during a song we played. After talking with her it was when I started playing "Flow My Tears" by Stu Hamm (this is a bass solo cover we did at every show). She just cried through the whole song and had an intense moment with God Almighty. She thanked me for helping her reconnect with God and went on her way. That night on my way home, I thanked the Lord my God for healing my carpal tunnel and giving me this opportunity. I realized that this band could be used for God's glory.

It was becoming more clear what God's vision and plan was for me and this band. I just remember I was blown away that night on what God did. We prayed and He responded, we proclaimed Christ and people were touched by His Gospel. We believed we could be used to make a difference and He did the work, and His Name was lifted high. Even the band before us, who were blaspheming God, complimented us and wanted to know more about Jesus. When the Presence of God shows up and the Holy Spirit gets involved things happen. Seeds were sown that night and hearts heard the Gospel of Christ Jesus.

Another One Moving On

After our show in Stanton, our lead guitar player Tom unexpectedly decided he needed to move on. This was a real bummer because he was such a huge asset with his writing, arranging, and performing on stage. But I respected his decision to move on. As I thought it through, I wanted to replace him right away and recut all of the solo work he did on the project. What he did sounded great, but I wanted to have the guitar player who cut the tracks to perform live with the band.

Chris knew a guitar player who was looking to join a band, Jacob. His style was a little different than what Liquid Eclipse's music was, but I felt in my spirit he would be a good fit. We had to recut the solos as soon as possible because the songs were ready to mix. Jacob and I would have these marathon sessions where we would take on recutting the solos. We mic'd his amp and then he would come into the engineer room with me, and I would coach him through the songs. He had ideas as to what to do but we recorded the final cuts section by section in the studio.

Then we came to the song "Only Love Remains" and something special happened that night. It was the last song to lay down a solo. I had Jacob do a dry run through the solo section a few times before we recorded it. Then I looked at him and asked if he was ready. There was this moment where we paused and took a 5 second breather before I hit record. I hit record, and I couldn't believe what I heard when Jacob came in with his solo. His first note of the solo captured my attention and immediately brought me into a deep feeling of God's love for me. It was one of those moments I will never forget. As he continued to play the solo, it was like angels were right there making sure what Jacob played was meaningful and impactful.

The end of the song is 3 minutes of Jacob's epic solo, and the amazing vocal arrangements Mark and Chris came up with. This was such an amazing finale to a great album. It was probably the best music, arrangement and lyrics that I wrote and co-wrote of any album. Jacob's solo capped this album off nicely. Needless to say, this was a Spirit-filled solo and I was so blessed to experience this time recording it as the Holy Spirit was working through Jacob.

We Claim to Be Christian Band

Now we are ready to mix down the project and send it off for mastering and print. I was the one who was mixing the songs with the help of other band members. It was good to have extra sets of ears and extra hands for moving sliders. This studio did not have automation for mixing so we had to do it old school. We start mixing the songs. They were all coming together great.

The Holy Spirit started putting that in my heart as a possibility of making Liquid Eclipse a Christian rock band. I would think about what happened in the Stanton, Michigan battle of the bands, and how God showed up that night. When Mark brought us together to pray in Stanton, it was like something switched on inside my spirit. Then the response to the answered prayer and the Gospel being proclaimed was amazing. It made sense in my brain to become a Christian band if what happened in Stanton would happen in other places.

I could relate to everyone there because I used to blasphemy God Almighty and party hardy. I knew what it was like to cover up the loneliness and emptiness of the world with self-absorb desires. I was lost with no hope until someone proclaimed the Gospel to me. I thought to myself, why couldn't Liquid Eclipse do the same? We could be used by God to bring hope to the lost and those who are hurting.

All of these events ignited a fire in me to want to be used by God to proclaim Jesus Christ through music and lyrics. It's like I couldn't get the sweet taste of the Good News of the Gospel out of my mouth. I just wanted to proclaim the Gospel to those without hope and searching for an answer to their emptiness. I thought to myself "that is what I want to do." I wrestled with the idea during the recording process of the album asking God for direction and how to do it.

I'll never forget the night Mark and I were mixing the song "I Believe In You" and we took a break to rest our ears. Out of the blue, Mark started talking to me about this idea of being a Christian rock band. Like to actually market ourselves as a Christian rock band. He pointed out how the lyrics could easily be pointed to God like we did in Stanton. He also pointed out that the lyrics are about searching for something and that something would be God and His love, mercy, and grace. He was right, and what he said confirmed what the Holy Spirit has been putting on my heart.

Then the Holy Spirit put on my heart to do a voice over of a Bible Passage, 1 Corinthians 13:4-8, in the song "Only Love Remains." We realized that this was all the CD needed to be recognized as a Christian rock CD. That passage of Scripture tied it all together. I ended up recording that spoken Word of 1 Corinthians 13:4-8, and wouldn't you know, it fit perfectly over the musical bridge already recorded. After we mixed the song "Only Love Remains", we got the CD ready to send to press and print. What an Amazing God we serve!!

We had to change practice spots for the band. Mark was working at a church in Lapeer, Michigan, and he was able to work out for us to practice there. Mark and I talked about it beforehand, and we decided to let all the other band members know we are now a Christian band. We were all in the church, and I started to talk to Darius and Chris about this change, and they thought it was a good idea. I have to admit I was nervous about losing them to this decision. The two guitar players, Sam and Jacob, had other opportunities and commitments, so they ended up moving on from Liquid Eclipse the same time we came out as a Christian band.

I thought about who I could call after Sam and Jacob left the band. I ended up calling the guitar player Ben from the band I used to play in, Surreal. I explained to him what was going on and he thought that it would be a good idea to come on board. This was good news, because he was a Christian and was moving towards being a Pastor. We were able to get the talent and the heart after God, which was a win-win for us.

I Can Relate

My heart was breaking for the lost and those who feel as though they have no hope. I could definitely relate. Where I came from, myself being lost with no hope and scared, separated from my Creator. I used to party and give my attention and adoration to those bands who were anti-God and promoted Satan's kingdom. I became convinced that music influences people in a dramatic fashion. I experienced it myself growing up. When I saw what God Almighty, the Lord of Hosts, did in Stanton, I knew in my spirit that this band, Liquid Eclipse, could influence people with the Good News of Christ crucified.

Doing that show at Stanton was a game changer for me. I saw that God Almighty can do anything. That He is more powerful than His adversary Satan. That His Word will not come back void. I experienced what it was like to simply step out and be obedient and proclaim Christ with boldness. When Mark stepped up and led us in prayer, I realized that God was calling us on to do His work through the music and lyrics of Liquid Eclipse. **I realized that obedience is more important than people's opinion.**

Where I was when I was lost and where I am now, is just like the difference between darkness and light, as the Scriptures say. Being reminded that I came from a place of not knowing God Almighty and rejecting His love for me and embracing the ways of the world. Now, I am in the family of God because of what He did by sending His only Son to die for my sin. I want everyone to know who Jesus is and what He has done for me. Seeing those who were lost broke my heart, and I started to mourn over the sin that separates anyone from our Savior.

God showed me mercy, and I wanted everyone to experience this same mercy that He gave me. *"Once you were not a people, but now you are God's people; once you had not received mercy, but now you have received mercy."* 1 Peter 2:10 ESV. The Lord spoke to my heart as I was taking all this in, and He said to me **"The sinner is ignorant to my Word and doesn't know any better. A sinner sins because that is all they know to do. Give them the same mercy that I have given you and show them the same love that I have shown you."**

CHAPTER 7
"Ministry Begins"

"For the Son of Man came to seek and to save the lost."" Luke 19:10 ESV

Vision Changed

It was time for Liquid Eclipse to have our first rehearsal as a Christian band. As I was driving to this rehearsal, the Holy Spirit started to speak to my heart. My vision was always to get signed by a major label. Now, the Holy Spirit challenged me to shift gears and cast a different vision for the band. I kept hearing in my spirit these two words- *win souls.* I got really excited when 'win souls' came to my spirit and it brought out a passion and drive to see this happen. I settled in my heart now that we have claimed to be a Christian band, winning souls would now be a part of the gigs we do. As a matter of fact, it would be the primary goal and mindset that we have as a band. Win souls!

I then thought that if the vision is to win souls, what would the plan be to see this happen? The Holy Spirit took me to Hebrews 12 *"Therefore, since we are surrounded by so great a cloud of witnesses, let us also lay aside every weight, and sin which clings so closely, and let us run with endurance the race that is set before us, looking to Jesus, the founder and perfecter of our faith, who for the joy that was set before him endured the cross, despising the shame, and is seated at the right hand of the throne of God."* Hebrews 12:1-2 ESV. As I run the race with the mindset to win souls, I am simply supposed to fix my eyes on Jesus.

I then thought about what that meant to fix my eyes on

Jesus, and two concepts came to my spirit. The first concept to fix my eyes on Jesus was to stay in the Word of God. This was something I was already fired up to do and settled in my heart that I would continue to do no matter what. The Scripture that I read to help me understand to stay in Word of God was *"My son, do not forget my teaching, but let your heart keep my commandments,"* Proverbs 3:1 ESV. Along with the Scripture in the New Testament *"Let the word of Christ dwell in you richly, teaching and admonishing one another in all wisdom, singing psalms and hymns and spiritual songs, with thankfulness in your hearts to God.* Colossians 3:16 ESV

Both of these Scriptures are encouraging to me and calling me on to *keep* the Word of God and let it *dwell* in me. This means to not merely read the Scriptures to gain a worldly knowledge but rather heed to Scriptures. And because I have a heart set towards God, I will be obedient to the Scriptures. I knew I would have to keep the Word of God in my spirit if I was to obey the Lord. I would read the Scriptures daily and I would memorize certain passages of Scripture as well. This was a great way to get it into my spirit and keep it there. Besides, I saw through the whole New Testament that Jesus and the Disciples quoted the Old Testament from memory all the time. I figured if they did it, so should I.

The second concept of fixing my eyes on Jesus was prayer. I had already been learning how to pray according to the Word of God. This type of prayer though, would be more of a boldness to make war against the enemy- that being Satan. Or you could word it this way: I would pray to be able to stand against the devil and his schemes. I would pray for boldness to proclaim Christ. I would pray that the Word of God would take root in the hearts of anyone who heard the Gospel through Liquid Eclipse. I had to expect Satan would try and stop me at every point and try to dismantle the band. But I also know that I served a God who is Mighty and is my warrior as the Lord of Hosts and would fight every battle for me. **I knew the only weapon available to me was the Word of God and Satan could not stand against what God**

spoke through His Word.

Ephesians chapter 6 would be my go-to passage of Scripture to memorize and live out. *"Finally, be strong in the Lord and in the strength of his might. Put on the whole armor of God, that you may be able to stand against the schemes of the devil. For we do not wrestle against flesh and blood, but against the rulers, against the authorities, against the cosmic powers over this present darkness, against the spiritual forces of evil in the heavenly places. Therefore take up the whole armor of God, that you may be able to withstand in the evil day, and having done all, to stand firm. Stand therefore, having fastened on the belt of truth, and having put on the breastplate of righteousness, and, as shoes for your feet, having put on the readiness given by the gospel of peace. In all circumstances take up the shield of faith, with which you can extinguish all the flaming darts of the evil one; and take the helmet of salvation, and the sword of the Spirit, which is the word of God, praying at all times in the Spirit, with all prayer and supplication. To that end, keep alert with all perseverance, making supplication for all the saints, and also for me, that words may be given to me in opening my mouth boldly to proclaim the mystery of the gospel, for which I am an ambassador in chains, that I may declare it boldly, as I ought to speak."* Ephesians 6:10-20 ESV.

I made up my mind that I would not back down to anything that would hinder the message of the Gospel. Within my mind and the vision of the band I would not be ashamed of the Gospel of Christ crucified. *"For I am not ashamed of the gospel, for it is the power of God for salvation to everyone who believes, to the Jew first and also to the Greek."* Romans 1:16 ESV. I am so glad that the Lord Almighty, through the Holy Spirit, showed me all of this before Liquid Eclipse started on this new venture with a renewed vision and plan. The focus on winning souls for His kingdom set the tone for this band's ministry to succeed.

This revelation of the new vision and new plan led to knowing what the purpose of this band was going to be - proclaim Christ crucified. This is why this band exists, to proclaim Christ. Now as a band we understood what was expected of us. Vision to win souls, a plan to fix our eyes on Christ Jesus, and our purpose as to why this band exists is to proclaim Christ Crucified. We are now ready, and the stage is set, so to speak.

Songs From Two Bands Merge

As we started rehearsing, we realized that we had a lot of music to perform if we wanted to. With Darius and Ben in the band we could do Surreal songs. As Ben and I talked about it we decided to add both "Child of Glory" and "Of Sea and Sky" to the Liquid Eclipse set. Ben also wrote songs called "Rapture" and "Sinners Song," so we added those as well. Now as a band we could perform for an hour and a half to two hours. We threw in a few cover songs, and we had ourselves a dynamic set list for live performances.

Darius took it upon himself to put together a backdrop that was about 20 foot long and 7 foot tall. What he did was airbrush the Liquid Eclipse CD cover onto a black backdrop. This was such a great addition to the show. Made us look that much more professional. Mark then stepped up and put together a light show which was amazing as well. I researched and bought a PA that would be able to handle all of our shows. It was big and loud, and we had plenty of PA power as a rock band. It was awesome to see the members of the band pull together to make this band that much more appealing and professional by raising the standard for our shows.

Because setting this equipment up was a huge task, we had to hire roadies and a dedicated sound guy. We asked Berry to join our band as the sound guy. He was a friend and an amazing Christian so when he said yes, I was happy to have him on board. Berry really did need someone to help him, so I asked my good friend Dan, who was also a Christian, to fill that need of being Berry's helper. Dan would end up doubling as my bass roadie as well. He was my bass roadie during my Surreal days so he was already familiar with my set up and how I like things done. I always used different basses for live performance, so having Dan doing both rolls was a blessing.

Dan was not only a good friend of mine, but he was also a singer songwriter as well. We would spend time hanging out and writing songs together. Sometimes Dan, Micah, and I would have fun putting lyrics and melody to some acoustic guitar riffs I wrote at Micah's pad. It was always a good time when the three of us would hang out. When not at Micah's pad, Dan and I would work on many songs together at my place. Songs like "Send Me Your Love," and "Come Lord Jesus." They were all acoustic guitar driving songs because that is the instrument I was focusing on to write songs with lyrics.

Liquid Eclipse ended up being quite the production. With the size of our PA and light show, having consistent extra hands was important. Everyone was a part of this ministry and all of them had a part to play to put on a successful show. It's a true statement: A sound-man can kill a show. It wouldn't matter if the band Liquid Eclipse performed our best show, if the sound guy is not competent then the show can come off bad. But Berry and Dan made sure the shows come off amazing so ministry could go forth. Everyone was set in place, and we were all doing our part bringing our gifts and talents to go on this journey of proclaiming Christ Crucified. And away we went.

Just a Spark

Mark and Ben took on the responsibility of booking gigs for the band. They both had connections to churches and other venues for us to perform. It didn't take very long for us to get out there and start performing. Our first gig was like we have been playing together for a long time. It just all fell into place and clicked. Word of mouth traveled fast, and churches were getting a hold of us to come play.

Some churches wanted us to play for their congregation

and some wanted us to play at outreaches they were hosting. Either way, we proclaimed Christ Crucified. The Bible says in Mark 16:15 *"And he said to them, "Go into all the world and proclaim the gospel to the whole creation."* Mark 16:15 ESV. It says to proclaim the Gospel to everyone, not just the lost. All of creation. Which means everyone whether they are saved or not. One of the things I learned is that church goers need to hear the Gospel just as much as the lost. Some going to church were not even saved.

I learned that it is not up to me to decide who should hear the gospel when we would perform live shows. I saw everyone as a candidate to hear the gospel and be changed. The Holy Spirit really helped me understand that I was to be a sower of the seed, which is the Word of God. And as I sow the seed, I am not to be concerned where the seed ends up, but rather be obedient to simply sow the seed.

Some Fun Times Gigging

We ended up doing a lot of gigs and traveling all over Michigan. There was this one gig we did up in Alpena, Michigan that I'll never forget. We were invited to play this event at a church on a Saturday night. So, we packed up our show and headed up there. We got there and the church was beautiful, and the people were great. We got all set up and were ready to go. There was another event at this church already going on when we got there, so there were a lot of people there mingling.

Mark noticed a lot of older people from the other event sitting down in the pews where our concert was going to be. These people had to be in their seventies. Some of them had canes. Now, we are a heavy metal progressive rock band who always plays for a younger audience. When we as a band saw an older crowd sitting down, we became very concerned as to whether or not there was a miscommunication as to what kind of band we are. We didn't want there to be any false expectations.

    We talked to the event coordinator, and he reassured us that he knew what he was getting and didn't want us to make any adjustments to our show. He encouraged us to go out and do our show as normal. With that said, we cranked it up and went out there and loudly proclaimed Christ as a progressive hard rock band. There was one older gentleman who stuck out in the crowd among the other older people. He was four rows from one of our speaker stacks and was jamming to every song. His foot was tapping, and he even raised up his cane from time to time to let us know he approves of this loud music for the Lord Jesus. Christ Crucified was proclaimed and people of all ages were touched at that gig.

    There is another funny story of a gig we did at the Res Life Church. The stage where we set up was too small for all the equipment that we had. We had to be creative to have everything of ours on stage. Chris would normally hold the switch down for our fog machine at the very beginning of the show. I told him I could do it this time because the foot switch ended up in my area.

    We started every show with our song Can You Feel the Power. There is this fast bass lick in the beginning to start the song off. I started the song as usual and hit the switch to the fog machine to let out a little fog like we normally would do while doing this intro. No problem so far. Then I stop and the whole band comes in together with this intro riff. I picked my foot up like I normally do and then I brought it down to the downbeat as the band came in. Then I usually close my eyes and bow my head down till the verse comes in. Well, I opened my eyes to find all I could see was fog from the fog machine. I couldn't even see my other band mates on the stage. That's how foggy it was. What happened was, when I put my foot down after the intro riff, I put it down on the fog machine foot switch without realizing it. Which filled the whole room with fog.

    Chris was trying to get my foot off the switch, but I couldn't hear him because of the loud music on the stage. Well, needless to say when the fog cleared out of the room the people who were in the room when we started the song were cleared out as well. I don't blame them because fog from a fog machine has a very distinct odor and is an annoyance. It was still a good show and by the end of the night we were talking to people about Jesus and selling some of our merchandise.

Growth and Opportunity

The song After the Rain caught on with some listeners. It was the most radio friendly song on the CD. This song started to put Liquid Eclipse on the map and get us much airplay and CD sales. Also, it was gaining the attention of some record labels. This was very exciting for us as a band. We were getting airplay even as far as the Philippines. We even had international sales of our CD too. There was a distributor called Rad Rockers who picked up our CD and bought 300 copies to sell through their catalog. We were their top CD seller in their catalog for a while. Things were moving along for sure.

We started to receive offers to tour with other bands. One of the offers we got was touring with Night Ranger for 2 months on the west coast. We turned it down because there was a personal conflict with some band members. We had another offer to go tour Europe for a few months. Chris's wife was pregnant and the day we would've left she was due. Family first. Chris being home for his wife and child was more important. We also could have warmed up for Dream Theater at the Capitol in Flint, Michigan. But again, there was personal conflict to keep us from doing that as well.

Some might speculate that we should've done these opportunities regardless of band member conflicts. But we are a Christian band with biblical standards. I wasn't about to put that kind of pressure on band mates to cause strife in their families. What kind of leader would that have made me. Also, in hindsight this was God's protection from us getting away from our vision which was to win souls. We would not have been able to do that touring with other bands. We stayed the course and let the Holy Spirit lead us where to go.

Davison United Methodist Gig

Mark worked as a youth Pastor at United Methodist Church in Davison, Michigan at the time Liquid Eclipse was together. There was a huge youth event his church was hosting, and they needed a youthful band. Liquid Eclipse was a perfect fit. They were expecting several youth groups to show up, so we had to make sure we were on top of our game.

The event was all afternoon, so we had to come up with three hours of music. We had a solid two hours already down because that's what our normal show was. Mark asked Ben and I if we could each do a solo acoustic set before Liquid Eclipse went on. Ben had no problem with this because he already did this kind of thing. I accepted, but was very nervous about it because I have never done an acoustic set and sang in front of an audience. So, this would be challenging for me to do.

The day of the gig arrives, and we set up our sound equipment along with our light show. Dan made a point to be at this show because of the importance of it. He was such a huge help setting the PA up with Berry. After helping with that, Dan did what he does so well and made sure my basses were set up and in tune. He just didn't tune my basses; he would actually do the setup for them if it was needed. Bass setups are no easy task in the middle of a show. Dan was great at doing this. And for this show, it was definitely needed.

So everything is finally ready to go because of our awesome support from Berry and Dan. I started the show with three songs I wrote on acoustic guitar. Then Mark joined in and did his own solo set on his keyboard. Now if you knew Mark you would know that he loved Michael W. Smith. So of course, there were songs from Michael W. Smith in his set. Within Mark's set he did an original that talked about fanning the flame. The Holy Spirit brought this to my spirit to ponder and learn about later on down the road. Mark had such great original music. Then Ben wrapped up the solo sets with his stellar acoustic set.

Now the stage was set for Liquid Eclipse to come out and put on a show. This would end up being one of our best shows that we performed. As a band we just seemed to be hitting on all cylinders this day. As usual Dan as my bass tech was spot on and in sync with me. It was just refreshing to have him hand me my bass when I would switch, and it would be in tune and sound amazing.

When I looked out at the audience, it was awesome to see the youth being engaged with what we were doing. You could say Liquid Eclipse rocked their face off and Christ Crucified was proclaimed. This was a memorable gig and God Almighty used this gig to encourage us as a band to keep doing what we are doing. Kids were impacted by the music that day. There was a lot of fellowship with the kids and we made a great connection.

Saginaw

We got this call from a church in Saginaw, Michigan to come and perform at their youth event. We of course said yes. Then we were told that a record label was specifically coming to the show to see us because they heard many good things about our music and us as a band. Now this was a pleasant surprise for us as a band. I've never had a record label come out to a gig to scout us out.

At this gig we were warming up for an upcoming Christian band out of Detroit. The word was this band was nervous that we were going to show them up. Apparently, there was such a strong (what the industry calls a) 'buzz' going on about Liquid Eclipse, that word was we were a noteworthy band. People were remembering us and talking about us which felt amazing to know this.

We got up to Saginaw, and because there were two bands who use their own equipment, we had to figure out how to share the stage with their set up. Just meeting the other band, I could tell there was some tension. We decided to help ease the tension so it would not be difficult. Darius talked to the other drummer and they both ended up using his kit for both shows that night. That was a common thing to do so the sound man could have less of a headache between bands. I even let the other bass player use my bass rig as well. We tried connecting with the other band and figured everything out, so we were good to go.

Somehow, I ended up doing a few acoustic songs before we went on. I ended up doing the song Hear Me that night. I have been performing this song by myself for a while now and I was trying to find the sweet spot for it live. I got done playing my couple songs, and to my surprise my girlfriend Christi, my future wife, told me that the song, Hear Me, ministered to her. Something clicked in her and she said it was a time with the Lord and His love mercy and grace. That alone made the night worthwhile.

It is close to the time we were going to start. Something just felt off the whole night. Between us as a band, we seemed distant, and there did not seem to be the expectation of a good show like we would normally have. I don't know if it was nerves or what was going on. Maybe it was the fact that there was a record label there to scout us out. Ben and Mark met the reps and then let the rest of the band know who they were so we could make sure to shake their hand after the show. I'll never forget the look on the other band's face before we went on. It was like they were expecting us to make them look bad and they were not wanting to go through this experience.

We were five minutes from going on, and for some reason I decided that I did not have to tune my bass. There was a rift between a few of us on stage right before we started as well. Again, something felt off. Mark asked me if I tuned my bass, and I told him I'm good, my bass doesn't need it. That was an arrogant comment to stay. As a pro bass player, I should always tune my bass no matter what.

It's showtime. The lights come on and Chris pumps the crowd up and I go to hit my first note to start the show and I just felt my fingers stiffening a little. Because of that I really could find the timing of the intro riff. Then when the whole band came in, I noticed one of us was noticeably out of tune. I just couldn't believe someone in our band was out of tune. It was either Ben's guitar, Mark's keyboard, or my bass. I was convinced it was one of them. Now I'm distracted on stage, and I start to go over and tell Ben to tune his guitar. I even went to Mark to make sure he was playing the song in tune.

Whoever was out of tune became a huge distraction for me. I was not focused on giving God the glory and proclaiming Christ through the music. I was concerned about the looks and the performance of the band instead of relaxing and allowing God to have His way. As I listened to see who's out of tune on the next song in the set, I realized that it possibly was me. Then after the second song I realized 100% it was me out of tune. This frustrated me even more. I tried to tune it by ear to Mark's keyboard in between the second and third song. It just made it worse. Because I'm playing the songs out of tune, it was causing Chris to sing flat. Which was causing the background vocals to sing out of key as well. It was like no one on stage was in sync harmonically with instruments or vocals.

We get to the part of the show where we go into this bass tapping song -I Believe In You- and what a mess. I tried to tune my bass again, but it didn't work. I got to the part where I do my fast-tapping bass solo and it was so far out of tune and to top it off Darius was missing the double kick on the part as well. I was embarrassed and devastated after that song. I looked like an incompetent musician, and I felt as though I let the whole band down.

The second half of the show was not as bad as the first half but our opportunity to impress this record label was now gone. We got done with our set and the tension between us as band members was intense. Mark immediately went to the bathroom and Darius disappeared as well. I really didn't know what to do so I tried to avoid people and started to pack up my basses. The record label reps talked to Ben for a minute and then I saw them shake hands and say goodbye.

When the other band was coming onto the stage to set up for their show, they all had smiles on their faces. They knew we didn't have a good night. As a matter of fact, it was the worst Liquid Eclipse concert ever. They were gracious to us though and tried to say good job, but we all knew it was terrible. They ended up having a great performance and overall God was glorified that night.

I had a lot of questions that night for God Almighty. I asked Him why everything fell apart, and our opportunity was lost. I really thought that the Lord was going to use this opportunity to get us signed to a major label. All of us in the band thought the same thing. What happened? Nothing went right at all. God Almighty, in His love, quieted my spirit and simply put in my spirit that He did not want Liquid Eclipse to be signed. That we were exactly where He wanted us to be.

When He put this into my spirit, I realized something. I had to be okay with where God had me and not always be looking for something better. I had to be ok with performing at locally-based churches and events and stop worrying about getting to the big stage and tour the world. What God has given me to do is enough for me and I told myself that I don't need more. Only what God has for me. This night uprooted inside me of what was left of wanting to be signed. The Holy Spirit said to be content with proclaiming Christ and where He takes us as a band. We would learn to be content with what God gave us to do as a band ministry.

We Were Laborers

We continued to do the work of the Lord through this band. In the practical sense we did good business. We showed up on time and followed through with an outstanding show, and then spent time with the people there to be available to talk about Christ our Lord. By this time in the band's journey, every band member was comfortable talking about Jesus and praying with those who wanted prayer. We would make sure we kept the focus on Jesus and not ourselves, so His name was glorified.

We would pray before every show and call down the strongholds of Satan so that the testimony of God's love, mercy and grace would be understood. I firmly believe that prayer is the foundation to evangelizing and proclaiming Christ. I saw in the Word of God that the Apostle Paul was always asking for prayer that he may be able to proclaim Christ with boldness and have the opportunity as well. We would make it a habit to pray the same thing before every show. This would help us stay focused for the show and remind us that the Holy Spirit is there to do the work and we are simply the vessels to be used to get His work done.

We Sowed the Seed

I would always tell my testimony in the middle of each show we did. In the beginning of us being a Christian band the testimony was how I had joy and peace after I was saved and healed of my carpal tunnel. But that evolved into presenting the Gospel how I realized I was a sinner and God the Father came after me and saved me from my sin and healed me in my mind, body, soul, and spirit. How I was once lost, dead in my sin, and now I am redeemed and a new creation because of Christ Crucified.

Chris was led by the Holy Spirit to minister the message in certain songs to the audience throughout the show. We focused on pointing everyone to Jesus and fixing our eyes on Him. Our message became a message of God's Love for us and how He died for us and saved us from eternal separation from Him. Chris understood as a front man that we were there to sow the seed of the Word of God. Nothing more and nothing less. Show after show we would throw the seed of the Word out with the faith that it would take root and grow at some point.

At the end of the evening, we would offer a time for people to connect with God and encourage everyone and anyone to come and talk with us afterwards. We ministered as the Holy Spirit saw fit. People were saved. Chains were broken. The enemy was pushed back, and people were set free from their sin. All the work of the Holy Spirit. Glory to God.

God Protected Us

We did a lot of one-on-one ministries after each show, and I am so grateful for that. I believe if we would've been signed to a major label, we would've missed out on the ministry that we as a band were able to do. I came to understand that we were protected by God the Father from being signed. There was opportunity but God had His reasons for shutting those doors. Instead, he kept us right where He needed us to be and allowed us to minister the saving Gospel of Jesus Christ to people who needed it to hear it. Our God is an amazing God!

We Said Our Goodbyes

There came a time that came where all of us as members of this ministry knew it was time for it to end. I started this band in 1993 and it had a good 5 years of giving God glory and sowing the Word of God. I talked to Mark about what I was feeling in my spirit about dissolving the band and he agreed it was time. After talking privately to the other members about this, we all agreed that it was the right thing to do. It was as though it ran its course and was time to move on.

Mark suggested that we all get together and say our goodbyes. With that in mind, we set a time to meet at Darius's house. As we all remembered the good times we had as a band we laughed, we cried, and told a lot of stories. It was a good thing, and we all knew it was right. We ended by holding hands in a circle and all of us took our turn praying for each other and thanking God Almighty for the opportunity to minister the Gospel to His people. We said our goodbyes, hugged each other and went our separate ways. This was the end of an amazing ministry that God Almighty allowed all of us to be a part of and for that I am thankful.

P.S.

Mark ended up getting a phone call from EMI records in 2002 asking if our band was still together because they wanted to sit down and talk about giving us a record deal. This contact was from the record label seminar in Flint that we attended back in 1995 and gave all record labels present our CD to listen to. EMI records was one of them present. They said they had just listened to our songs and really liked them and wanted to talk. God does have a sense of humor, doesn't He? By this time the band had moved on to starting families and moving out of state, and we all had different lives. I mean it was 7 years after we gave them our CD and bio and they finally just listened to it. I had to laugh at the timing of all of this. But, once again, God knows what He is doing. He protected us from chasing after a dream that was not in His vision and plan. Thank you, God the Father, for protecting, guiding us and leading us in the way we should go. *"I will instruct you and teach you in the way you should go; I will counsel you with my eye upon you."* Psalm 32:8 ESV

CHAPTER 8
"Landmark Lanes"

"Blessed be the God and Father of our Lord Jesus Christ! According to his great mercy, he has caused us to be born again to a living hope through the resurrection of Jesus Christ from the dead," 1 Peter 1:3 ESV

God Knows What He Is Doing

When I started my band Liquid Eclipse in spring of 1993, I also did a job change in August of 1993. I switched the bowling alleys I worked at from Colonial Lanes to Landmark Lanes. It was time for a change, so I took the job as the B Mechanic night shift at Landmark Lanes. They had a reputation for being a bowling alley where the best bowlers would bowl at. I was definitely excited to be a part of this culture because I took my bowling seriously and actually wanted to go pro at one point. This job switch was good all the way around.

My supervisor was a buddy of mine from school, and we worked together at Colonial Lanes for three years. His name was Luke. When I got there, Luke started to show me around and explain how he wanted the lanes maintained. Landmark Lanes had a reputation of having what they call a 'shot.' A shot is how the lanes are oiled. Luke had a system of how to put out an amazing shot so the bowler's game scores would be higher than other bowling alleys in the area. It would be nothing for the men's league on Friday night to shoot six 300 games in one night. Bowlers loved bowling at Landmark because they knew they would have an amazing shot to work with.

Then Luke took me back behind the lanes to show me what us mechanics call the 'pit'. This is the mechanic's shop area where I would sit and wait for the upfront desk to give me a call over the intercom system to go fix any of the lanes that broke down. We went into the pit, and it is a tiny room about 10' by 25.' There was no heat, and it wasn't very clean either. But nonetheless, it was the area for me to sit and wait for any of the lanes to break down. Knowing I was going to be working by myself, I concluded that I would be spending a lot of time in this pit area.

I Had Time to Pray

I realized after working a few nights at Landmark that I had a lot of time on my hands. As I thought about it, I figured while I am at work waiting for a lane to break down, I could read the Word of God. The next day I brought in my Bible to read. After the first week of reading the Bible, I found I could read for hours while working in the pit. This was so awesome, and my love for the Word started to become stronger. This pit area would become my sanctuary as I studied the Word.

I thought to myself that I might as well pray in the pit area as well. I mean I was by myself so what better time than when I'm by myself. I would make a prayer list of people to pray for and their needs along with my needs and desires as well. In making this list I could keep track of how God answers the prayers I lifted up to Him. During that time of prayer, I would lift my co-workers up to Him and ask for their hearts to be prepared to listen and receive the Gospel of Jesus Christ.

I found out quickly that since the pinsetters were so loud while they were running, no one could hear me as I prayed. I could walk behind those pinsetters and yell as loud as I want when I pray, and no one would know. Because of that, it allowed me to be myself when I pray and helped me be more confident.

I was developing my prayer personality and style. Which you could say was a more aggressive and militant mindset.

I really started to take the idea of memorizing Scripture seriously so I could pray them over family, friends, and myself as well. I was convinced that praying Scriptures over others and my life was a sure way to get answered prayer. God cannot go back on His word, and it will never come back to Him void. As I read the Scriptures, I came across a lot of prayers that the Apostle Paul would pray for his readers along with asking for his readers to pray certain things for him.

The one Scripture that the Holy Spirit put on my heart to start with was Colossians 1:9-14 *"And so, from the day we heard, we have not ceased to pray for you, asking that you may be filled with the knowledge of his will in all spiritual wisdom and understanding, so as to walk in a manner worthy of the Lord, fully pleasing to him: bearing fruit in every good work and increasing in the knowledge of God; being strengthened with all power, according to his glorious might, for all endurance and patience with joy; giving thanks to the Father, who has qualified you to share in the inheritance of the saints in light. He has delivered us from the domain of darkness and transferred us to the kingdom of his beloved Son, in whom we have redemption, the forgiveness of sins."* Colossians 1:9-14 ESV.

I would memorize this passage of Scripture by reciting one sentence at a time over and over. I would also write it out on paper from memory as well. This would help the Word get inside my spirit. I didn't wait until I had it memorized to pray it over people including myself. I would have my Bible in hand when I would go to pray. I was developing the habit of having my Bible in my hands as I prayed to the Lord Almighty.

I learned that I could make the passages of Scripture that I was praying for others personalized. Within the passage, every time there was the word *you,* I would insert someone's name in place of *you,* and when I prayed it over myself, I would insert the word *me.* For example, the passage of Scripture I mentioned above in Colossians 1:9 *"asking that you may be filled with the knowledge of his will in all spiritual wisdom and understanding"*- You can put someone's name in place of the word *you* or insert the word *me* which is referring to yourself. I started to develop this approach to prayer and would pray the Scriptures over Luke, my supervisor.

Luke Is Drawn to Jesus

Once in a while, Luke would come back to the pit area and hang out after he was done working his shift. We would talk about work, how to make things better on the job, and about things going on around us. He would always catch me reading the Bible when he came back to talk. I could tell he was interested in knowing more about the Bible. It was like he wanted to ask questions, but something was holding him back. I would continue to pray for Luke.

Then the time came when Luke started asking me questions about what the Bible says. I only had about a year and a half of reading the Scriptures, so I had limited knowledge. But I was willing to share what I knew at that time from the Bible and do the best I could to answer his questions. I had to remember that it really didn't matter if I was to give a quick answer or have a long conversation. Either way, the Holy Spirit was going to work through me to plant seeds of the Word of God into Luke's heart.

As Luke was asking questions in the pit, I was learning that sometimes a one sentence answer is sufficient. I always felt that every time someone asks questions about the Bible, I would have a three-point sermon ready to preach to them. I had this mindset that I had to be as thorough as possible to make my point. As I talked with more people, I learned that too much information can be counterproductive. It was hard to give concise answers to his questions, but I had to try and do that. I was even learning that it's ok to say that I didn't have the answers to some questions: 'I don't know, but I'll find the answer to your question and get back with you.'

Proclaim With Boldness

This is the time the Holy Spirit was going to challenge me to proclaim Christ Jesus with boldness. It kept coming to me to follow the model of how Peter proclaimed Christ in the Book of Acts. He made it very simple: Christ was killed on a cross and then He was resurrected; and death does not hold Him down. *""Men of Israel, hear these words: Jesus of Nazareth, a man attested to you by God with mighty works and wonders and signs that God did through him in your midst, as you yourselves know— this Jesus, delivered up according to the definite plan and foreknowledge of God, you crucified and killed by the hands of lawless men. God raised him up, loosing the pangs of death, because it was not possible for him to be held by it."* Acts 2:22-24 ESV. The Holy Spirt was prompting me to be bold and proclaim Christ crucified and resurrected. To not be afraid to call Luke on to repentance. Simply say the words and let Him, the Holy Spirit, do the rest. I then started to pray for the confidence and courage to do what the Holy Spirit wants me to do.

Then the time came when Luke started asking about how he could know Jesus. I fell out of my chair because it took me off guard, but I collected myself and thought about it for a second and then shared what the Holy Spirit put on my heart. Christ crucified and resurrected is what came into my spirit to say. Then He encouraged me to be bold. I remember saying to Luke how his sin is forgiven and how death is defeated. Then I told him he could know Jesus if he repents and turns from his ways and asks Jesus to forgive his sin and confess Him as Lord. An intense burning came over my body while I was saying this to Luke and when he left the pit area the burning intensified even more as I started to praise God. That was an amazing night in the Lord.

The Holy Spirit was gracious and was able to use what I said to Luke. I learned that **the Holy Spirit is more concerned**

about the heart and passion of what you say, rather than the correctness of what you say. Let your passion for people to know Jesus dominate and don't let lack of experience hold you back from proclaiming Christ Crucified. I had the expectation that God was going to do something in Luke's life.

A short time after that conversation with Luke, he came back to the pit as usual one night. He was agitated and started to tell me how God was nothing and He will do nothing for him and do nothing for me. He picked up my Bible and said to me "What is this going to do for you?" and then threw it aside on the workbench. He said a few more things to me and stormed out of the area. I initially didn't know what to think. One night Luke was asking how to know Jesus and now he was saying God is nothing and will do nothing. This broke my heart. My first thought was to pray for him and ask God to forgive him and not be upset with him. So, I prayed. I also asked God to protect Luke, that he would come to know Jesus and come back to the Lord. I couldn't get mad at him because I knew he was wrestling with questions like I did.

Luke ended up disappearing shortly after that night for about a week. No one knew what was going on with him or where he went. I had to work a lot to cover his absence from work. I was praying that he was ok and nothing bad happened to him. The next thing I know the pit door opens and it's Luke. I was very surprised but thankful he was ok. I thought he was fired or something, but he went on to tell me he is now saved, and Jesus is the Lord of his life, and he wants to learn more about Jesus. My jaw hit the floor and I did not know what to say. Before, he was railing against God and now he wants to know this God who saved him. Hallelujah! The Holy Spirit did something in Luke's heart and brought him back to Jesus. I was amazed at what the Lord had done. Praise the Lord and Lift up His Name!!

After Luke was done talking to me the Holy Spirit got my attention to make sure that I understood something. The Holy Spirit reminded me that He was the one who gave me the opportunity to sow the Word of God into Luke's heart. I just made myself available and spoke what I believed the Holy Spirit wanted me to say. I had no idea how God was going to make the seed take root, but He made it take root and I am thankful. A brother brought back to the Lord. Amen!!!

I have shared with people my testimony of being healed and how good God is. I have even shared with others what the Bible says to the best of my ability. But with Luke, it would be the first time ministering the Gospel of Christ Crucified and resurrected. I never thought I would be able to do this, but the Holy Spirit was there teaching me and prompting me to be bold.

After Luke gave his heart to Jesus, I realized that maybe I really am an evangelist at heart like was spoken over me at Holy Cross Church. It just seemed to be my passion and desire to see everyone know Jesus. The intensity of the Holy Spirit made me thirst for more of His presence. I always had in my heart to preach the Gospel and after this experience it was stoking that fire inside of me and I was gaining confidence to speak boldly.

2am Bible Studies

Luke and I started to get together at his place after I got out of work for Bible studies. This would be the beginning of our own small group. I was learning from Holy Cross that small group Bible studies are a great place to be discipled and grow in the Lord. I was stoked to get together with Luke and study the Word of God. I thought this was the coolest thing in the world having a study partner who was developing into a great friendship as well. Mind you it was after I got out of work at 2am, but I didn't care because this was exciting.

We had been doing Bible study for a time, and the next thing I knew, Luke said that someone else was going to be at the Bible study that night. I thought to myself this is great, the more the better. I went over to his place and the new person was Luke's new girlfriend, Kate. Kate was a waitress in the nightclub attached to the bowling alley. Now Kate wasn't saved when she came over, but, over time and continuing to study the Word, the

Holy Spirit did a work in Kate's heart, and she is now a part of the Kingdom. Praise the Lord!

I Meet Christi

The Bible study is now up to three. Mind you we are still getting together 3-4 times a week. As time goes by, Luke tells me that Kate is bringing her roommate over for Bible study that night. I asked Luke who it was, and he told me her name was Christi and that she too is a waitress in the nightclub attached to the bowling alley. I couldn't picture who this was.

Luke jogged my memory by saying "Dude... remember she was the one who asked you for the ink spot remover."

I responded, "Oooohhhhh. I remember her now."

I initially met Christi before she came to Bible study that night. As my memory was being jogged, this is how I remembered who she was. Someone up in the nightclub connected to the bowling alley, spilled ink on themselves. I got this call in the pit to go meet this waitress up on the concourse. I'm making my way up to meet her, and I look up and see all this glitter on her and in her hair. She was beautiful, that's for sure. I instantly became nervous as I walked up to her.

She looks at me and asks, "Do you have anything like ink spot remover?"

I responded by saying, "Ink spot remover. Not sure what you mean."

I thought to myself what the heck is she talking about? I ended up telling her I did not have anything like that. She said OK and then turned around and went on her way.

I was instantly attracted to her because she had jet black hair and green eyes. I've always wanted to be with someone like that and that someone just talked to me. After that interaction I did what any mid-twenties guy is supposed to in this situation. I decided to go up into the nightclub and sit somewhere where I could stare at her. I was just that drawn to her. This would go on for a while, and honestly it probably was freaking her out because she took note that there was a psycho guy staring at her in the bar. I was just *that* drawn to her, that I wanted to check her out. I am a people watcher. I can learn a lot about someone by just watching them and how they interact with others. Needless to say, when I realized it was her showing up to Bible study that night, I was more than thrilled it was her.

    We would do many Bible studies together after that night. As time would go on, Christi and I would develop a wonderful friendship. Luke and Kate were already on their way to getting married so during and after bible study Christi and I would be able to get to know each other more and more. I found she had a peaceful spirit about her. She was strong and not afraid to take anything on. She loved to laugh and would make me laugh all the time. We would joke around a lot, and we seemed to have the same sense of humor. My mind could relax when I was around her.

    We ordered food from Starlite Coney Island as usual, and they would wrap the food boxes with these huge rubber bands. One night we were goofing around, and she grabbed one of those rubber bands and somehow made this person out of it by stretching it between her fingers on both hands. Like a rubber band puppet. Then she would go into a character voice, and we would carry on funny conversations with who she called 'rubber band man.' It became a thing for us to do after Bible studies once and while. It would always make me laugh and put me in a better mood.

    A few months later as we were wrapping up our Bible study, Christi was all excited to have me watch this music video on the TV in Luke's living room. I went in there to watch this video by Big Tent Revival, the song is called "Two Sets of Jones.'" The song lyrics compare 2 couples, one were the Jones' who start out their married life with the foundation of money and what seems to be security, and the other set of Jones' start out their married life with Jesus being the foundation, relying upon God to make a way. Christi is super excited while this video is playing and tells me she wants to be like the Jones' relying on Jesus as their foundation. This spoke volumes to me, and I would tuck this information inside my heart.

The Breakup Transition

With all this going on I was having a lot of emotional issues with my girlfriend. After three years we ended up having too many frustrations, and it seemed like the best thing to do was break up. So, she broke up with me. I was devastated at the time. The night she broke up with me I went over to Christi's place crying my eyes out. I didn't know who else to turn to at the time. All I know is I was so relieved when she opened her front door. She gave me a big hug and let me cry on her shoulder. It was at this time that I realized that maybe God was trying to bring her and I together. But it was going to take time for me to heal before I could jump into another commitment.

The next day I started to pray that God would heal my emotions and bring balance to my thinking again. I started to realize that maybe God placed Christi in my life for more than just being Bible study partners. There was peace when I was around her and I felt content knowing that we could take on the challenges of life together with Jesus leading us. God ended up giving Christi an experience and told her to wait for me. As I remember Christi saying, it was like a dream/vision where there was an audible voice telling her to wait for me. God knew I was going to need time to heal and get my mind straightened out.

Even though God told Christi to wait for me and endure this situation, she was running out of patience. I can't blame her after all she had been waiting for a few months. While she waited there was this guy who kept asking her out at the bowling alley that we worked at. He was asking her out for a longtime and Christi would always politely decline his offer. His name was Roger. His birthday was coming up and all he wanted was to go out on a date with Christi for his birthday. Christi, being frustrated with me, agreed to hang out with Roger for his birthday. He went over to her place to pick her up, and Christi invited him inside so she could give him a cake she baked for him. He went inside her place and sat down, then all of a sudden, he became very sick to his stomach and had to leave right away. They did not finish the date. Come to find out later on that night the stomach pain went away soon after he left, and he was ok. I do not think that was a coincidence, but rather God was keeping Roger away from Christi.

It had been four months since my breakup, and I was still dealing with my confused emotions and balancing them out. I was having a hard time dealing with my ex-girlfriend moving on and it was causing so much stress in my life. I was a mess. I knew my feelings for Christi were more than friends. On Thursday, March 20, 1997, when I was at work, I had a mental breakdown. I was angry and felt rejected and I was at the end of my rope. I was already praying about this to God my Father, and I just wanted to have my emotions balanced so I could get on with my life.

I just burst out into tears and my knees hit the floor and I cried out to God to take this emotional burden from me and bring peace to my mind. I told God I couldn't take this emotional stress anymore. No sooner than that got off my lips it was like I could feel the weight actually being lifted off my shoulders. Instead of being hunched down I was able to straighten up. I heard an audible voice say, "Get up". I got up and then I heard the voice say, "It is done, you are fine now." It was like my emotions over this matter were no longer torturing me. My mind was clear, and I felt like I was set free from emotional bondage. Praise God!! God had to heal my emotions so I would be ready for a new relationship with Christi.

I remember thinking to myself that I had to go and talk to Christi. I had to tell her that I was ready to commit to a relationship with her. I thought maybe I should go pound on her door, but it was 4am in the morning. Thursdays were late nights for me at the bowling alley and Christi probably wouldn't appreciate me pounding on her door at 4am is my guess. I knew she would be working the next morning. I thought to myself, I'll see her in the morning and tell her I am ready to be with her. I was stoked big time!!

The next morning, I got myself ready and headed up to the bowling alley to talk to Christi. At this point she quit being a waitress and became the bowling alley cleaning lady. I hardly slept the night before because I was so excited to talk to her. On my way there I was going over in my head how to say I'm ready to start a relationship with her. So many ways to say it. I got there and asked the counter help where she might be, they said she was cleaning the bathrooms. I checked all the bathrooms except one and thought she had to be there. I thought "Ok here I go..." I'm nervous but I get ready to open the door to the men's room thinking about how I'm gonna say this to her. I opened the door to the bathroom and there she was holding a toilet brush.

I said the first thing that came to my mind, "So, was I worth the wait?"

She gave me this look and said, "What are you talking about you psycho".

Sometimes saying the first thing that comes to your mind is not the best idea. I don't remember what we said after my grand entrance in the bathroom, but I do remember we went out to lunch at our favorite spot, Starlite Coney Island, and talked about the future things we wanted to do together.

Being A Good Boyfriend

A few months go by, and Christi ends up going to the ER because she is having pains in her abdomen. I head up to the hospital to be a good boyfriend and support her. This was something pretty serious, so they admitted her. I remember sitting on the end of her bed after they gave her some demerol to manage the pain she had.

She said, "Thank you for being there for me."

I said to her "That's what it is all about, speaking of which, how's the first weekend in May sound?"

She said, "For what?"

I casually said, "for our wedding."

She answered, "Ok."

What a romantic I am, ain't I? Kicking in bathroom doors and saying, "so was I worth the wait" and then asking her to marry me while she is in the hospital drugged up on demerol. But she said yes! We set our wedding date for May 9, 1998.

CHAPTER 9
"BREAK ME"

"Your boasting is not good. Do you not know that a little leaven leavens the whole lump?" 1 Corinthians 5:6 ESV

Arrogance Stinks

Soon after we set the wedding date, seeds of arrogance started to be exposed within myself. Even though the Lord was giving me opportunity to proclaim Christ and be a part of fruitful Bible studies, hints of arrogance were popping up. Something didn't feel right in my gut when I was being that way, but I would let it go and not do anything about it. I would make sure I had an excuse for me to say and act the way I did. I honestly thought it was part of the process of growing in the Lord. I had no idea how deep this root of arrogance had become.

It started out with I noticed that my friends were not really wanting to hang out with me as much. There seemed to be a stand-offish attitude towards me from my friends. I could even tell that my family was avoiding conversation with me about God and the Bible. It seemed that is all I wanted to talk about. Or maybe I should say I wanted to hear myself talk about it. I remember thinking that I was getting good at memorizing the Bible and being able to rattle off several Scriptures on command. I always looked for an opportunity to show off what I knew to people during conversation and prayer.

It was like this knowledge was feeding a need that I had to

feel smart and have something that no one else around me had. I never felt smart while growing up. I was a good reader, but I never finished reading a book. I didn't try very hard in school so I only got average grades. When people would talk to me, I had a hard time understanding what they were saying when they would use more complex words. I even had a hard time understanding some everyday words. But then when I started to memorize the Scriptures and became good at firing off Bible verses and being able to recite it with chapter and verse, it made me feel like I could do something intellectually that no one else around me could do. It made me feel accepted amongst friends and peers.

With my friends and family, I didn't know how to speak the Word of God with discretion and love. And because I misused the Word of God due to my arrogance, I became a judgmental Christian. I didn't even realize that I was being this way. I would judge people for their wrongdoing and justify my actions thinking I was acting this way in the Name of God. I really thought everyone else was the problem and I was always right. This attitude did not display the love of Christ Crucified at all.

This knowledge made me feel like I was above others, I would be very critical of people. Because of that, I became blind to people's emotional status and what they needed. I would end up telling others what I thought they needed to hear and feed the stench of arrogance within myself. This is a trap that I fell into because of my own fault. **Knowledge can very easily make someone feel like they are on a pedestal and puff up the heart with pride.** *"Now concerning food offered to idols: we know that "all of us possess knowledge." This "knowledge" puffs up, but love builds up. If anyone imagines that he knows something, he does not yet know as he ought to know. But if anyone loves God, he is known by God."* 1 Corinthians 8:1-3 ESV

Knowledge leads to arrogance when just left to knowledge. In my blindness I became more interested in obtaining a 'knowledge' of the Scriptures so I could impress people with my 'knowledge' like I was somebody. I would volunteer my friends and family against their will to listen to my thoughts on what I was studying from the Bible at that time in my life. Some would give me grace and sit and listen, which encouraged me to keep doing it whenever I saw them. After a while, I noticed most would become irritated with me and some would even start avoiding me. It was obvious that I was puffed up on knowledge and I was stinking up the place with my arrogant attitude as I told everyone what I knew, whether they wanted to hear it or not.

Two Friends

God will get your attention through some of the most unexpected ways. That's what He did with me. I was having dinner with a friend and of course I started talking about God and Jesus and the Bible. He had knowledge of Scriptures, so I was trying to impress him as I did with anyone else. We were talking about the existence of God and he was challenging the credibility of God's Word. Of course, I was trying to beat him over the head with all I knew and trying to convince him to come back to God. He stopped and looked at me and told me how arrogant and shallow I was.

Of course, I'm offended, and I tried to defend myself and kept firing on the Scriptures to him.

Then he stopped me again, looked right at me and said, "If I was ever to be a Christian again, I would not want to be like you."

I was hurt by this statement. It was like a bombshell going off and really rattled me. I had to take an honest look at my walk with God and try to understand why he would say that to me. I didn't realize I was being perceived that way. I would never want to push anyone away from knowing Jesus. But this friend perceived me as being shallow and arrogant. My walk was not displaying the love of Christ but instead a judgmental critical Christian. I needed to hear this.

Another friend spoke the truth to me as well. I needed help getting one of my cars from my place of work. I called a close friend to come and help me. When we talked on the phone, I could tell something was bothering him that day. But he came over, picked me up, and we went to pick up my car. I needed him to follow me in case the car overheated. We made it back to my place with no issues. He said he had to go but of course I started talking to him about the Bible and trying to convince him that he needs to go back to church. Like always I started this conversation without asking. I was firing scriptures at him that had no meaning to the conversation except to make me feel superior. He was irritated as I was spouting off and allowing arrogance to once again stink up the place.

He stops me from talking and looks right at me and says, "You are so arrogant".

I was offended and defended myself saying, "No I'm not! You just can't handle what God is telling you."

He just kept saying how arrogant I was and drove off. After that night we really didn't talk too much and then eventually we lost touch. I lost him as a friend. He was right though, I was arrogant.

God Draws Me to Repentance

After those two conversations I had to consider what they were saying. I was hearing from other sources that my group of friends did not want my overzealous, enthusiastic, bible-thumping mindset around them. There were leaders within my church family that told me to my face that I was so arrogant that they wanted to punch me in the nose. There were just too many people all saying the same thing. I really could not sweep this under the rug and say that all of these people were wrong that were saying I was arrogant.

I decided to take this to the Lord in prayer. I ask Him to examine me and to see if there were any offensive ways in me (Psalm 139:22-23). I asked Him that if there was any arrogance in me that He would show me my wrongdoing. Because I was trying to memorize as much Scripture as possible, I was aware of the Scriptures where we as Christians are supposed to examine ourselves. *"Examine yourselves, to see whether you are in the faith. Test yourselves. Or do you not realize this about yourselves, that Jesus Christ is in you?—unless indeed you fail to meet the test!"* 2 Corinthians 13:5 ESV. I knew Jesus Christ was in me, but I knew in my spirit that I had to examine myself closely. I had to admit that maybe all these people were right in saying that I was arrogant. I needed to have this confirmation from the Lord though. In my mind I really thought I was doing something in the name of the Lord by forcibly telling people about the Bible.

The Holy Spirit opened my eyes and I started to clearly see my arrogance. Other conversations were brought to my memory of me bulldozing friends with the Word of God. I started to realize that they were enduring the conversation and were in no way listening to what I had to say. I thought to myself "doesn't everyone have to hear the Word of God? Shouldn't I be telling everyone about the Bible?" This way of thinking would justify in my mind that I needed to tell everyone about the Bible no matter what. What I was actually doing was trying to guilt people into going to church and coming to Christ by using Scripture to point out their wrongdoings. I would directly or indirectly try and guilt them into believing the way I believed. When they resisted what I was saying, in my arrogant mind I saw their resistance as being a part of Satan's kingdom. I would then spew out tons of Scripture to try and make them feel even more guilty of their separation from God.

There was a conversation brought to my memory of when Liquid Eclipse was doing gigs. We did this gig at a church in the Detroit area. We put on a real solid show that day. I didn't have any roadies at this gig, so I had to set up and tear down myself. I was not in a good mood for some reason. There were voices antagonizing me and for some reason I was allowing that to get to me. I knew in my spirit that there was an arrogance in me that day and for whatever reason I did not care. I was in a mood. The coordinator of this event came and found me and said there was a young man who wanted to talk to me when I was done tearing down. Normally I would be ecstatic but for some reason this time I was mad about it.

I took my time and was hoping I could just slip out unnoticed. The young man actually approached me as I was putting my bass in its case. He started talking to me and giving me kind words of encouragement about my bass playing. He said my testimony of God healing my carpal tunnel was impactful. For some reason I was taking all this in and not giving the glory to God. It was like there was something on me. Then he started to ask questions about playing bass and how I got to that level of bass playing. I told him that practice was the key. But I said it in a very condescending way. He seemed excited about that. Then for whatever reason I told him that if he practices a lot then someday, he might be as good as me. Then I gave him an arrogant smile. He gave me this look of I can't believe you said this to me. Then he turned around and walked away with obvious disappointment.

It was like I was happy that I acted that way and said the things that I did and was glad he was out of my hair. I finished packing up and left. I remember as I was driving home the Holy Spirit convicted me of what just happened. He was convicting me for being rude and arrogant. I felt so terrible. I turned around to go find this young man and apologize for the way I treated him. When I got there, it was too late, he was gone already. I went home asking God to forgive me for my arrogance. I had no idea why I was acting that way. Was it just my sin nature? Was it a demonic attack? Either way I spewed arrogance on that young man and did not minister to him at all. I prayed that God would not let this arrogance affect the young man and that he would grow to be a mighty bass player for His Glory.

Mindset of a Pharisee

As I continued to struggle with arrogance the Holy Spirit showed me that I was in the mindset of a Pharisee. Pharisees would always try and show off how religiously correct they were. They would pray and fast where everyone could see them. They would seek the front seats of honor. They would have a mindset that the sinner was below them and they would separate themselves from the sinner. It was like they had a mentality of us and them. There is us, the spiritual, and them, the not so spiritual. I saw others not as spiritual as I was, and I would see them as being below me.

That was actually my mindset. Just like the parable of the Pharisee and tax collector. *"He also told this parable to some who trusted in themselves that they were righteous, and treated others with contempt: "Two men went up into the temple to pray, one a Pharisee and the other a tax collector. The Pharisee, standing by himself, prayed thus: 'God, I thank you that I am not like other men, extortioners, unjust, adulterers, or even like this tax collector. I fast twice a week; I give tithes of all that I get.' But the tax collector, standing far off, would not even lift up his eyes to heaven, but beat his breast, saying, 'God, be merciful to me, a sinner!' I tell you, this man went down to his house justified, rather than the other. For everyone who exalts himself will be humbled, but the one who humbles himself will be exalted.""* Luke 18:9-14 ESV.

Another Scripture that came to my spirit was when Jesus was eating at Simons house, and he was trying to pull Jesus into this arrogant mindset by pointing out that He was allowing a sinner to touch Him. *"One of the Pharisees asked him to eat with him, and he went into the Pharisee's house and reclined at table. And behold, a woman of the city, who was a sinner, when she learned that he was reclining at table in the Pharisee's house, brought an alabaster flask of ointment, and standing behind him at his feet, weeping, she began to wet his feet with her tears and wiped them with the hair of her head and kissed his feet and anointed them with the ointment. Now when the Pharisee who had invited him saw this, he said to himself, "If this man were a prophet, he would have known* *who and what sort of woman this is who is touching him, for she is a sinner.""*Luke 7:36-39 ESV. I really saw those who didn't confess Jesus as Lord as being less than me. Even if they did confess Jesus as Lord, I would make sure they knew that I was better than them because of all the Scripture I could call out from memory.

Arrogance is a heart issue, and it manifests through words and making others feel less than. I became good at this and justified it in the name of telling others of the Bible. Just like the Pharisees when they were trying to stop Jesus and His disciples from spreading the Good News. They, the Pharisees, were the ones on top of the religious intellect. So, when Jesus came on the scene and the people were amazed by His teachings, the Pharisees lost their mind. They figured they had to get rid of Jesus and His radical ideology. They were so arrogant that they couldn't humble themselves and see the Savior right in front of them. This is how it was with me. I loved Jesus, but I was irresponsible with the emotional hurt and needs of His people. I used His people to make myself feel smarter and superior. Woe is me. Help me Jesus.

Sorrowfully Convicted

Then the Holy Spirit took me to this Scripture *""Judge not, that you be not judged. For with the judgment you pronounce you will be judged, and with the measure you use it will be measured to you. Why do you see the speck that is in your brother's eye, but do not notice the log that is in your own eye? Or how can you say to your brother, 'Let me take the speck out of your eye,' when there is the log in your own eye? You hypocrite, first take the log out of your own eye, and then you will see clearly to take the speck out of your brother's eye."* Matthew 7:1-5 ESV.

I read this passage of Scripture many times before, but this time I stopped and had a knot in my gut. I could not deny that I was acting just like an arrogant Pharisee by thinking I was superior to others, the way I treated them, the things I said to them, always judging and pointing out their faults and not paying attention to my own faults. I was so upset that I allowed this mindset to take root in me.

I became sorrowfully convicted of my wrongdoing and this really affected my walk with the Lord. One of the things I was convicted of was the fact I pushed people away from the Lord. I realized that He put me in a sphere of friends and family who needed to hear the Gospel proclaimed clearly. I felt like I blew it and messed everything up. How could I be so arrogant to those around me? I was so disappointed in myself. I took the precious Word of God and used it to build up my own self and puff my head up with knowledge. I felt like I should apologize to people for being an arrogant jerk.

Another conviction from the Holy Spirit was that I gave God Almighty a bad name. I did not represent the kingdom of God in the right way. I became someone I didn't want to be, and I felt like I let God My Savior down. After I was saved and healed, I was overwhelmed with joy and genuinely wanted everyone to know what the Lord Christ Jesus did for me. I felt I represented the kingdom of God in a genuine way. But at some point, things changed, and I started to become critical and judgmental which led to this arrogance. I allowed false teaching to work its way into my spirit and take root. *"Your boasting is not good. Do you not know that a little leaven leavens the whole lump?"* 1 Corinthians 5:16 ESV

Thank God Almighty that He does not deal with us according to what we deserve, but instead is rich in mercy and His love is steadfast. He came and reassured me that He loves me and has not forsaken me. As it says in Psalm 51, David acknowledges his sin and repents of his wrongdoing. I used Psalm 51 as my model in Scripture to ask God to forgive me of my sin. *"Have mercy on me, O God, according to your steadfast love; according to your abundant mercy blot out my transgressions. Wash me thoroughly from my iniquity, and cleanse me from my sin! For I know my transgressions, and my sin is ever before me. Against you, you only, have I sinned and done what is evil in your sight, so that you may be justified in your words and blameless in your judgment. Behold, I was brought forth in iniquity, and in sin did my mother conceive me. Behold, you delight in truth in the inward being, and you teach me wisdom in the secret heart. Purge me with hyssop, and I shall be clean; wash me, and I shall be whiter than snow. Let me hear joy and gladness; let the bones that you have broken rejoice. Hide your face from my sins, and blot out all my iniquities. Create in me a clean heart, O God, and renew a right spirit within me. Cast me not away from your presence, and take not your Holy Spirit from me. Restore to me the joy of your salvation, and uphold me with a willing spirit."* Psalm 51:1-12 ESV.

Just like the Psalmist David, I asked God to cleanse me, wash me, purge me and make me clean. I begged God to not cast me from His presence. This was agonizing for me. After praying through this Scripture with the Lord, He restored me and forgave me for mistreating his creation with the stench of arrogance.

This Broke Me

The next day I started to ask the Lord to help me be better and to not become arrogant ever again. I asked Him to help me understand His love and mercy and grace. Then I prayed Ephesians 3:14-19 over me *"For this reason I bow my knees before the Father, from whom every family in heaven and on earth is named, that according to the riches of his glory he may grant you to be strengthened with power through his Spirit in your inner being, so that Christ may dwell in your hearts through faith—that you, being rooted and grounded in love, may have strength to comprehend with all the saints what is the breadth and length and height and depth, and to know the love of Christ that surpasses knowledge, that you may be filled with all the fullness of God."* Ephesians 3:14-19 ESV

I believed that God Almighty would do these things that I asked for, especially if I was praying His word. I just wanted to know His love for me like Ephesians 3 asks. I wanted Him to pick me up and give me a fresh wind of His Holy Spirit and ground me in His love like Ephesians 3 asks. I asked Him to please give me a heart that is after His heart, and a love that is for his creation. I asked him to let me see people through His eyes and not my eyes. That I could look past the sin and learn to love the person and not pay attention to the sin in their lives.

Working at a bowling alley there would be tons of opportunity to see people through the eyes of Jesus. I then started to be purposeful in looking at someone the way Jesus would. Even though they would cuss and make crude jokes, I had to learn how to ignore the sin and look at the heart of God's creation.

Friday Night Conversations

There was a young man who bowled on Friday nights men's league that I became friends with. He had the same struggles I had before I was born again. Drinking, drugs, sex, cussing etc. The Holy Spirit opened my spiritual eyes and showed me that he doesn't sin just to sin, but his sin is a result of what he has been through. We talked about this in our 2 am Bible study. Christi brought up the point that people act a certain way because there is something they are dealing with. Some kind of traumatic experience or roots of bitterness or maybe someone abused them and hurt them. **Behavior is a result of the experience.** With this in mind, I was able to not be offended by his sin.

I came to realize that this young man was sinning out of ignorance. He did not know any better. He had no understanding that what he was doing was wrong. He just went about his life thinking this is what is normal. As I thought about that, even if I was to point out his sin, it would do no good if he didn't realize he is a sinner and is separated from God. I've been through this myself before I was saved, and Regine looked past my sin because I was doing it out of ignorance. Now, it is my turn to be the one to set aside the sin and display mercy while loving the sinner. The Apostle Paul talks about this same thing in his letters, *"though formerly I was a blasphemer, persecutor, and insolent opponent. But I received mercy because I had acted ignorantly in unbelief,"* 1 Timothy 1:13 ESV

As the weeks go on there was one Friday out of the blue this young man asked me about what he called that "Bible stuff." I was more than happy to sit and talk with him about this. He had a lot of questions about God's love, sin, and why Jesus had to come to earth and die on the cross. This was a wonderful conversation and I ended up praying with him on the spot and told him we would continue this conversation. He struggled a lot with the concept of how God could love someone like him. I put him on the top of my prayer list for the week with the expectation we would talk the following Friday.

The next Friday comes, and the opportunity was there for us to have another awesome conversation. This would actually go on for several Fridays after he was done bowling. This young man opened up and shared how his dad was abusive and was not a father to him at all. He shared with me how he struggles with the idea of being lovable and had a lot of baggage with his dad. My heart broke for him because his lifestyle was a result of one man hurting him and leaving a hole in his heart. In conversation, he became very angry towards his dad and started cursing him. I had to calm him down and show him that our Heavenly Father is not like any earthly father. That our Father is love, mercy, and grace.

It was amazing because there would be no one around to distract us while we had our conversations. This was unusual for a bowling alley at 9pm on a Friday. He was popular and there was always someone wanting him at the bar afterwards or head to the casino. Then one Friday he asked me how he could get to know Jesus. I was so overwhelmed with joy that he wanted to know Jesus. I told him it was as easy as what the Bible says – confess Jesus as Lord and believe that He was raised from the dead. A few weeks later he gave his heart to Jesus. Amen Lord,

Hallelujah!

Seeing Through His Eyes

I started seeing God's created people through the eyes of His love. I ask the Lord to break my heart for the people around me anywhere I go. That I may see their hurting heart and set aside their sin. My desire to preach the word in a ministry setting was starting to come to the surface more and more. And because I started seeing God's created people through His eyes of love, I wanted to reach the masses with His love, mercy and grace. Then the Holy Spirit took me to this Scripture *"Thus says the Lord: "Heaven is my throne, and the earth is my footstool; what is the house that you would build for me, and what is the place of my rest? All these things my hand has made, and so all these things came to be, declares the Lord. But this is the one to whom I will look: he who is humble and contrite in spirit and trembles at my word."* Isaiah 66:1-2 ESV. I would spend a lot of time meditating on the passage as the Holy Spirit would keep in front of me to be broken before the Lord. I realized that **brokenness leads to being able to minister Christ Crucified to the lost and dying.**

I decided one day at work that I would attempt to go through my shift without sinning. Now of course this is impossible, but I wanted to try it as if it were an exercise. I asked God the Father to help me fix my eyes on Him and that I would see His Creation through His eyes. I asked Him for a love for others like I never had. To overfill me with the Holy Spirit and that His Presence dominates my being. I ask him to purge me and cleanse me from any sin that I know of and any sin I was unaware of. I prayed this Scripture over me *"Who can discern his errors? Declare me innocent from hidden faults. Keep back your servant also from presumptuous sins; let them not have dominion over me! Then I shall be blameless, and innocent of great transgression. Let the words of my mouth and the meditation of my heart be acceptable in your sight, O Lord, my rock and my redeemer."*

Psalm 19:12-14 ESV.

I had the most amazing work experience. I stayed in prayer and kept quoting His Word wherever I walked that night. Whenever I did sin in thought, word or deed I asked for forgiveness right away. I really tried hard to stay focused on seeing the hearts of those around me that I was working with. I was amazed how it was easier to keep my mind focused and not allow the carnality of others to bring out my sin. Of course, I sinned, there is no way anyone can be without sin. The Bible says, *"If we say we have no sin, we deceive ourselves, and the truth is not in us."* 1 John 1:8 ESV.

I have to say it was a tremendous experience though. I went home that night having a whole new perspective of Christ Jesus being sinless His whole life. My thought was it had to be because He loved people with the agape kind of love and had no desire to entertain what this world had to offer. Satan offered Him the world and its kingdoms and Jesus quoted Scripture and told Satan to get behind Him. Jesus warns us by what he teaches in His Gospels to deny yourself and pick up your cross and follow him. I wanted to do that so bad. I was developing a stronger hate for sin and a stronger desire to serve Christ Jesus. *"And he said to all, "If anyone would come after me, let him deny himself and take up his cross daily and follow me. For whoever would save his life will lose it, but whoever loses his life for my sake will save it. For what does it profit a man if he gains the whole world and loses or forfeits himself? For whoever is ashamed of me and of my words, of him will the Son of Man be ashamed when he comes in his glory and the glory of the Father and of the holy angels. But I tell you truly, there are some standing here who will not taste death until they see the kingdom of God.""* Luke 9:23-27 ESV.

My prayer became: 'Lord Jesus, help me deny flesh and set a fire inside of me to boldly proclaim Christ all the time everywhere and anywhere. Use me, O Lord, and to bring souls into Your kingdom. Help me minister the Good News of Jesus Christ to the lost, broken-hearted and hurting. Keep your servant focused on You and You only. And take off my sin that so easily entangles me so I can run the race you have put before me. In Jesus Name. Amen.'

CHAPTER 10
"The Tongue"

"So also the tongue is a small member, yet it boasts of great things. How great a forest is set ablaze by such a small fire! And the tongue is a fire, a world of unrighteousness. The tongue is set among our members, staining the whole body, setting on fire the entire course of life, and set on fire by hell." James 3:5-6 ESV

Prayer - Tongues

The bowling season would always finish up around the end of April. Instead of being laid-off, I would still work at the bowling alley over the summers, but the schedule was lighter and there were no leagues. I typically would use the summertime to clear my mind. This one particular summer, the Lord took me into a season of refreshment and wanted to teach me some things that I have been praying for a long time. I wanted to receive the gift of tongues and learn spiritual warfare. I had to purpose my mindset to dig in and learn about these concepts that were put on my heart.

I have heard sermons on the idea of speaking in tongues. I have also heard people give their own opinion of what tongues is. It seemed that the more charismatic denominations of Christianity really emphasized the idea of speaking in tongues. Like it was a measuring stick as to whether you are a real Christian or something. Some denominations said it was of the devil and that tongues were only meant for the first century church. Others said that you needed to speak in tongues to be saved. There were just all kinds of opinions of what tongues were. Needless to say, it was confusing.

I had two experiences with the gift of speaking in tongues up to this point in my journey with the Lord. Not me speaking in tongues, but rather others speaking in tongues. The first one happened during the time I was dating Regine (1992). There was a young woman who worked at Subway in Flint, and she invited me to her church. Leading up to that, we always seemed to have conversations about the Bible. I ended up going to a service not knowing what to expect. The Pastor was vibrant, and the message was good as well. At the end of the service everyone in the sanctuary were praying and it was almost like the Pastor started stirring up emotions within the people there. The next thing I knew, everyone around me was speaking in tongues. This really freaked me out because it was something I never experienced. I had no idea how to respond, and I ended up leaving the service.

The second one happened just before I started doing this study on tongues (Spring 1997). The church Regine and Mark Siefert attended, Calvary United Methodist Church, were doing a pilot program for a Saturday night service. This service was designed to try and draw in what they called "seeker sensitive" people. It was a unique service with a mixture of contemporary secular and Christian rock music during the service. They wanted to see if the service would be a good long-term idea, so they hired me to lead this pilot program.

Christi and I were invited by the senior Pastor to come to a special midweek service and meet some of the musicians I would be working with. They were celebrating missionaries coming back from the mission field, so the place was packed. The service is moving along with lots of music and the people are shouting and singing and it was like being at a rock concert. I started to feel inside of me this uneasy feeling. The music was great, and the people were excited to be there, but I felt the Presence of God was missing. I made a point to tell Christi what I was feeling. I was actually mad about the whole thing. In my spirit, I started to tell God that He should show up and be a part of this service and that He should come down and be with His people. I couldn't figure out why God wasn't there. I actually wanted to leave the service.

As I was telling Christi that I wanted to leave the service the music stops and the people quiet down. Next thing I know, I heard a voice of a woman. I really couldn't make out what she was saying. People actually let her make her way to the front. As she spoke in a loud voice it was in a language I did not understand. She kept saying the same thing louder and louder, then she stopped and went and sat down. There was an awkward silence that came over the service. I looked at the senior Pastor and I saw him looking around at the people as if he was looking for someone specific. The next thing I know there is a man who gets up front and starts to say something as if it was God Himself saying it. He said "Some of you in this place think that I am not here. Some of you think that my Presence is not here. But I am here, I Am the Lord Almighty, and I am here in your midst and with all of you on this day." I broke out in tears and asked God to please forgive me. I felt terrible that I was so sure that the Presence of God was not there. Christi and I stayed for the rest of the service in the Presence of the Lord.

These were my two experiences with the gift of tongues before I started to do a deeper study of 1 Corinthians chapters 12-14. The first experience was tongues as in a prayer language. The second one was a corporate setting where one spoke the tongue and another interpreted. Again, I have heard all kinds of opinions of what tongues is. I had to clear my mind of all negative opinions and preconceived notions of what I was told and look in the Word of God to find out what the gift of tongues is. I prayed to God Almighty to please give me wisdom.

As I started reading 1 Corinthians chapter 12, I found confirmation of the corporate tongues. *"Now to each one the manifestation of the Spirit is given for the common good. To one there is given through the Spirit a message of wisdom, to another a message of knowledge by means of the same Spirit, to another faith by the same Spirit, to another gifts of healing by that one Spirit, to another miraculous powers, to another prophecy, to another distinguishing between spirits, to another speaking in different kinds of tongues, and to still another the interpretation of tongues. All these are the work of one and the same Spirit, and he distributes them to each one, just as he determines."* 1 Corinthians 12:7-11 NIV. Where it says in verse 10 *to another speaking in different kinds of tongues, and to still another the interpretation of tongues.* This is what I experienced at Calvary. I was glad to see that what it I experienced there was in the Scriptures.

The experience I had in 1992 was also in the Scriptures. As I continued to read, I found in chapter 14 much needed confirmation of what the Holy Spirit was putting on my heart. Even though I walked out of that service, I am glad I was able to experience that. I was exposed to hearing what tongues sounded like. It wasn't that I thought they were wrong, it was me not understanding what tongues are and I just got freaked out. I was ignorant to this teaching. Now the Scriptures say specifically that tongues build up the believer as in a recharging of one's spirit, and that the Apostle Paul says he wants all of us to speak in tongues. *"Anyone who speaks in a tongue edifies themselves, but the one who prophesies edifies the church. I would like every one of you to speak in tongues, but I would rather have you prophesy. The one who prophesies is greater than the one who speaks in tongues, unless someone interprets, so that the church may be edified."* 1 Corinthians 14:4-5 NIV.

Then I came to this Scripture *"For if I pray in a tongue, my spirit prays, but my mind is unfruitful. So what shall I do? I will pray with my spirit, but I will also pray with my understanding; I will sing with my spirit, but I will also sing with my understanding."* 1 Corinthians 14:14-15 NIV. That is what I was looking for. Confirmation that there is such thing as a prayer language. Praying in the Spirit and singing in the Spirit. I set my mind to press in and continue to ask the Lord for this gift.

As I meditated on those two verses my desire for tongues became stronger and stronger. I really didn't know how to receive this gift of tongues. I remembered reading in the Book of Acts how tongues were evident in the believer's life. First the day of Pentecost with the tongues of fire over each Apostle and then Peter preaches the first message post ascension of Christ Jesus and 3000 were born again (Acts 2 – full chapter). Then Peter was preaching the Word at Cornelius house and as he was preaching the Word the Holy Spirit came on everyone and they all spoke in tongues. (Acts 10 – Full chapter), specifically *"While Peter was still saying these things, the Holy Spirit fell on all who heard the word. And the believers from among the circumcised who had come with Peter were amazed, because the gift of the Holy Spirit was poured out even on the Gentiles. For they were hearing them speaking in tongues and extolling God. Then Peter declared, "Can anyone withhold water for baptizing these people, who have received the Holy Spirit just as we have?""* Acts 10:44-47 ESV. And finally, Acts 19:1-10, specifically verses 5 and 6 *"On hearing this, they were baptized in the name of the Lord Jesus. And when Paul had laid his hands on them, the Holy Spirit came on them, and they began speaking in tongues and prophesying."* Acts 19:5-6 ESV.

    I took these three passages of Scripture and meditated on them. The initial coming of the Holy Spirit in Acts 2 must have been an amazing day for the Apostles. Being filled with the Holy Spirit in an amazing way and boldly proclaiming Christ Crucified. The laying on of hands of Paul and the men in Ephesus receiving the Gift of the Holy Spirit was amazing as well. But the one that stuck with me was the preaching of the Word that Peter did at Cornelius house and how the Holy Spirit came on them and they spoke in tongues. I made the connection that the intensity of the Holy Spirit and the Word of God go together.

    I intensified my Word study time and took this matter to the Lord in prayer. I would pray every day for the Lord to give me the gift of tongues. The Bible said that the Holy Spirit gives the 'gifts of the Holy Spirit' as He sees fit. I knew there was a possibility that I wouldn't receive the gift. Knowing that, I pressed into the promises of the Scriptures even more. I reminded God that Paul said he wanted all of us to speak in tongues and that this desire in my heart had to be from my

Father in Heaven because He puts those desires in me. I would beg and plead with the Lord of Hosts to please give me the gift of tongues.

How I Received Tongues

One day I was in the pit at work, and a voice told me to go out of the pit back room and pray while walking behind the pinsetters during summer opening bowling. When you have 32 pinsetters running for open play it can be a little noisy. This was a perfect atmosphere for me to pray. Because I could get excited and be more vocal while praying and no one would hear me. I did what I was told to do and went out and started praying as I walked behind the pinsetters during league play.

As I am doing this, I get this strong desire to pray for the gift of tongues. Next thing I know there is a nervous feeling right in my gut and it started to work its way up to my mouth. But it stopped in my chest area and wouldn't go any further. The next day the same thing would happen. This would happen a few more times until one of those days that nervous feeling got up to my mouth. A voice said to stick my tongue out, so I did. Of course, I felt strange doing that, but I was trying to be obedient to what I was hearing. Still, nothing happened.

The next day I heard the same voice telling me to go and walk behind the pinsetters and pray. I was told again in my spirit to stick my tongue out, so I did, but this time I heard a voice say now speak, speak in the tongue given to you. I started to hear in my spirit a language I've never heard. I was trying so hard to make this happen and start speaking in tongues, but again, it didn't happen. I thought for sure I was going to do it that time.

I was frustrated I'll admit, and I thought maybe this was all in my head and fabricated by my own doing. Maybe those who said tongues is of the devil were right. The next day I started to get the urge again to pray for the gift of tongues. I was hesitant but I was reminded that it was God Almighty putting these desires in my heart. I went back out and walked behind the pinsetters while there was open bowling and started to pray to God the Father. That nervous gut feeling went from my gut to my mouth quickly and I heard that voice again say, "Now speak in the tongue given to you.' When I opened my mouth out came a word. I thought to myself "That was a tongue." I became excited. The voice told me to not stop, but to open my mouth and let out the living waters. I did, and I spoke a sentence in this given tongue. That voice said again, to open my mouth and not stop. When I opened my mouth this time a prayer language came out of me, and I started to speak in tongues. Once it started to come out of me, it wouldn't stop.

While I was speaking in non-stop tongues it was like I was preaching a message. Within my spirit I was speaking in tongues and within my mind I kept hearing the word freedom. As I looked around my eyes were open to the spirit realm and I could see a host of spirits, demons and angels, listening to what I had to say. It was driving the demons crazy, but the angels were rejoicing. It was like there was a battle of good and evil going on of some sort while I spoke in tongues. Either way, I was so thankful to receive the gift of tongues and was filled with joy. Thank you, Holy Spirit.

As I was developing this gift of speaking in tongues, I would definitely feel in my spirit that I was recharging as the Bible teaches. I also felt as though I was able to be in His Presence more often and to me it was like a form of communion with God Almighty. I always had fellowship with God Almighty every time I would read His Word. When I prayed, I felt a connection as well. But tongues, when I would pray in tongues, it was like I was right next to the Lord and in the secret place or Holy of Holies, so to speak. That's the only way I can describe it. It was a new experience for me to be close to God Almighty and be in His presence.

Visions From Tongues

Soon after I received the gift of tongues, I would get visions from the Lord. It was hard to grasp at first, but the Holy Spirit would confirm that what I was seeing was from Him and there would always be Scripture to back what was being seen in the given vision. I can't get into the details of these visions, because they were personal warnings for certain people in my sphere of influence. I can say this- what the Lord gave me in those visions He told me to write it down and give it to the person who was on my heart as I was having the vision. I have to admit, I was very nervous to do this. I had to completely trust the Lord that this was from Him and not my own doing.

Without disclosing the person or place, I can tell you this one- I had a vision cornering a Pastor I came to know. I saw that the Pastor had to make difficult decisions at that time in his church. There was a little more detail to it and then there was a Scripture in Ephesians that the Holy Spirit gave me to give him. I remember going up to his church to give him this vision that I wrote down. I was very nervous. I mean I thought who I am to deliver something from the Lord. Shouldn't this Pastor be able to get it directly from the Lord. But because I wanted to be obedient to the Lord, I gave this Pastor the vision I wrote down as I prayed in tongues.

I didn't hear from that Pastor for a while. Then about six months later, we ended up running into each other. We started talking and catching up on what each other was doing. Then he told me that the vision I wrote down and gave to him came to pass. He explained how there were five elders in his church that were always giving him problems and railing against him in every direction. Because of the details of the vision I wrote down and the Scriptures to back it, this Pastor was able to prepare himself for what these elders were planning against him. He thanked me for being obedient to the Lord and this vision was able to help him stop some real bad things from happening to his flock at that church. Praise the Lord!

I thought about why this Pastor wasn't getting this

knowledge through his prayer time with the Lord. Why did I have to get this vision from the Lord and then write it down to give to him. Then it dawned on me that the Lord wanted me to confirm what was already on this Pastor's heart. It's not that this Pastor was missing something from God. Rather, it was confirmation he needed from the Holy Spirit to have the confidence as to what to do to protect the flock that God Almighty has given him to shepherd.

Send Me

As I was praying in tongues again on a different day, I saw as clear as day a banner that had Isaiah 6 on it within my spirit. I kept praying in tongues and it just kept coming into my spirit. I reasoned that I should read that portion of Scripture. I then opened my Bible to Isaiah 6 and started reading *"In the year that King Uzziah died I saw the Lord sitting upon a throne, high and lifted up; and the train of his robe filled the temple. Above him stood the seraphim. Each had six wings: with two he covered his face, and with two he covered his feet, and with two he flew. And one called to another and said: "Holy, holy, holy is the Lord of hosts; the whole earth is full of his glory!" And the foundations of the thresholds shook at the voice of him who called, and the house was filled with smoke. And I said: "Woe is me! For I am lost; for I am a man of unclean lips, and I dwell in the midst of a people of unclean lips; for my eyes have seen the King, the Lord of hosts!" Then one of the seraphim flew to me, having in his hand a burning coal that he had taken with tongs from the altar. And he touched my mouth and said: "Behold, this has touched your lips; your guilt is taken away, and your sin atoned for." And I heard the voice of the Lord saying, "Whom shall I send, and who will go for us?" Then I said, "Here I am! Send me." And he said, "Go, and say to this people: "'Keep on hearing, but do not understand; keep on seeing, but do not perceive.' Make the heart of this people dull, and their ears heavy, and blind their eyes; lest they see with their eyes, and hear with their ears,* *and understand with their hearts, and turn and be healed.""*Isaiah 6:1-10 ESV.

After I read Isaiah 6, I couldn't get out of my head this vision that Isaiah was having in the temple of the Lord. I tried to imagine what it would look like to see the train of His robe fill the temple. And all of these heavenly Hosts saying Holy, Holy Holy is the Lord of Hosts. What an amazing vision. I thought to myself maybe that is what it will be like to be in the heavenly presence of the Lord Almighty. While praying in tongues, I was overwhelmed with His presence and would start to cry. I really didn't know why I was crying but I did know that I was in His Presence. I just had to take this in and bask in it for a while. Eventually, I found myself wore out from being in the Lord's Presence and wanting to go to sleep. This would go on for a few days in a row. I would pray in tongues and then read the Scripture of Isaiah 6 over and over and continue to be overwhelmed with the Presence of God.

Then one of these times of being in the Presence of the Lord, I realized that He was calling me on to go and preach the Gospel. I had a knowing in my spirit that He was calling me to preach the Gospel to those around me. I kept asking Him to send me. To send me where the lost are so I can preach the Gospel. But, as soon as I said send me, I was sorrowfully convicted of my sin. There were still some remnants of arrogance I was still dealing with, and it needed to be completely uprooted.

Power of the Tongue

Criticism and being judgmental is a result of arrogance, which is rooted in pride of the sinful nature and displayed through the tongue. The Holy Spirit took me on a study in the Scriptures about the power of the tongue. As I thought about the power of the tongue, what Jesus said came to mind: *out of the abundance of the heart the mouth speaks* (Matt 12:34). I believe that the Holy Spirit started to show me some thinking patterns that I needed to change to completely uproot the arrogance in me.

The first thing He brought to my spirit was how I used to openly condemn the church for not being up to the standard I thought they should be at. I would always point out how I thought the church was not spiritual enough and not walking in the Spirit of the first century church. I was very critical of most Pastors of today and thought that they were quenching the Spirit. Out of my arrogant heart came criticism of the Church. If I was going to preach the gospel, I cannot have this attitude towards God Almighty's church.

Also, the Holy Spirit also brought to my remembrance times I would be critical of others by pointing out their flaws and talking about them behind their back. I would stain their name and paint a negative picture of their person. Like the Scriptures say the tongue is a deadly poison which can destroy a person's life. My critical heart would make me believe that I should point out everyone's flaws. And in doing this, they would see their wrong and it would cause them to repent and turn from their sin. I thought this is what I was supposed to do. I was trying to guilt them into believing God Almighty was real. This is not biblical, and I had to change my critical heart and how I talk about, and to, the people around me.

The Scriptures confirm the damage the tongue can do. *"Look at the ships also: though they are so large and are driven by strong winds, they are guided by a very small rudder wherever the will of the pilot directs. So also the tongue is a small member, yet it boasts of great things. How great a forest is set ablaze by such a small fire! And the tongue is a fire, a world of unrighteousness. The tongue is set among our members, staining the whole body, setting on fire the entire course of life, and set on fire by hell. For every kind of beast and bird, of reptile and sea creature, can be tamed and has been tamed by mankind, but no human being can tame the tongue. It is a restless evil, full of deadly poison."* James 3:4-8 ESV. I had to stop being critical of God's church and His chosen Pastor's tending the flocks of God's people, and those in my life around me.

Then, the Holy Spirit placed on my heart to look at people through the eyes of Jesus. To see them as people who didn't know any better. Which would mean people are doing what they believe is right, based on their ignorance of God's saving grace. I was reminded that I once was ignorant to God's saving grace and the wretched sin I displayed was out of ignorance. Before I came to Christ Jesus, I thought what I was doing was normal and ok.

This revelation would lead me to realize that I have no right to criticize or judge anyone, knowing that I too am a sinner. Also, it is not my right to judge anyone according to the Word of God. That is for Christ Jesus to take care of on the Day of Judgement. I continued to ask God to help me see others the way He sees them and help me not be critical and judgmental.

Learn to Listen

Within a few days I found myself at work actually being able to interact with people without being critical of their sin. I found myself encouraging them with the Word of God and actually being able to listen to what they have to say without going on long winded sermons about the Bible. I was learning that listening is something that I had to work at because as the person would talk to me, I always wanted to interrupt them and say what I wanted to say. Learning to listen was very hard for me to do because I always liked to hear myself talk.

But nonetheless, I had to be very intentional to listen first, before I would say anything. I asked the Holy Spirit to help know when I should say something within a conversation. *"Know this, my beloved brothers: let every person be quick to hear, slow to speak, slow to anger;"* James 1:19 ESV. The discipline to listen first would be one of the hardest things I would have to learn. But with the help of the Holy Spirit, I could do this.

As I was learning how to keep arrogance in check and listen before I speak, the Holy Spirit drove home the point that both blessing and cursing cannot come from my mouth. *"With it we bless our Lord and Father, and with it we curse people who are made in the likeness of God. From the same mouth come blessing and cursing. My brothers, these things ought not to be so."* James 3:9-10 ESV. That my mouth should be seasoned with the grace of God and that the stench of arrogance needs to be buried under the grace of God as well. This would end up being one of the most valuable lessons I would learn. **To not be arrogant and condemn others. To see others as Christ Jesus sees them and listen with a graceful heart speaking only when needed.** To Him be the Glory.

"Let the words of my mouth and the meditation of my heart be acceptable in your sight, O Lord, my rock and my redeemer." Psalm 19:14 ESV

CHAPTER 11
"Visions"

""'And in the last days it shall be, God declares, that I will pour out my Spirit on all flesh, and your sons and your daughters shall prophesy, and your young men shall see visions, and your old men shall dream dreams;" Acts 2:17 ESV

Transition

Soon after I was married, the Lord put on my wife's heart to be a stay-at-home mom. At this time my wife was with General Motors for 3 years. She was the main breadwinner, and carried the insurance for our family. For her to be a stay-at-home mom she would have to quit her job at General Motors. This was a big deal because I did not have a formal education or experience to find a better job than what I currently had. At this time, I was still a bowling alley B mechanic, and I did music on the side. Both occupations did not provide enough to let my wife quit her job and stay home to raise our family. I had to take it to the Lord in prayer to trust Him for this transition.

I talked with my wife, and we agreed that as soon as I found something to support our family, she could quit General Motors. Before being able to search jobs via the internet, one would have to look in the newspaper Help Wanted ads for a job. I would pick up a Sunday paper every week after church and search the classified ads looking for a better job. One Sunday I saw an ad for pipefitter trainees. The ad said no experience necessary, and they would train me. The ad also said there was insurance and benefits offered as well. I applied for the job, went for the interview and got the job. I had no idea what a pipefitter did when I applied for the job. I mean, I figured it had something to do with pipe of course, but I really didn't know what I was getting myself into. I got the job just before Christmas, so they wanted me to start right after the new year of 2000.

My wife was getting anxious to quit GM. I told her to be patient and let me make sure this job was legit and everything they told me in the interview was actually true and not misleading. When I started the new job, I worked for about 2 weeks and asked a lot of questions. Then HR gave me the insurance package to fill out to be prepared when the insurance starts. When that happened and I realized what kind of insurance it was, I felt comfortable enough that this job was going to work out. With that said, my wife was able to quit her job at GM at the end of January 2000.

This was a big transition for me. The only job I ever had was being a bowling alley mechanic. I was comfortable and was used to the culture of the bowling alleys and loved that job. I also really wanted to pursue music as my career so my wife working at GM was perfect for what I wanted to do. I had to put my pursuit of music on the back burner after I found this pipefitter job with the hopes of a bright future.

I remember telling my Dad I got this job as a pipefitter and his eyes lit up and he was smiling ear to ear. I really didn't know what to expect. I soon learned that I was being trained to be what they call a Class 1-A pipefitter. I was going to learn how to bend steel tubing and build the pipe systems for production lines of the Big 3 Automakers. Once I realized that, the job became more exciting. I of course have to credit the Lord for this job transition.

Fanning the Flame

A few weeks go by, and the Holy Spirit starts fanning the flame inside me. My desire for the Word became stronger and my hunger for God increased and I found myself praying more often than usual. Then I was reminded of Mark's song "Fanning the Flame" from the United Methodist Church gig in Davison when my band Liquid Eclipse ministered there. Mark performed that original song of his and now the Holy Spirit was bringing it to my remembrance to minister to me.

If you have ever fanned a flame at a bonfire, the coals get hotter, and the flames become more intense. I just felt the Spirit burning and intensifying inside of me. It's like I had an expectation that God was going to set the place on fire with His Spirit. I didn't know what God's plan was, and that's ok, I just knew He wanted to do something at this new workplace and He was in control. The expectation I had created a knowing within me that I had to be ready to submit to His plan and the leading of the Holy Spirit. I started to become excited.

During this time, as my spirit was becoming more on fire, the Holy Spirit spoke to me gently as I prayed, and He made it clear that I am not to draw any attention to myself. He then instructed me to simply sit and read my Bible quietly. He also made it clear when I pray, do not make a show of it by letting others hear my prayers. When I read the Bible, I used a small pocket Bible and when I prayed, I made sure no one was around and that I was quiet about it in this shop. Nobody needs to know what you are praying about- just you and God with the Holy Spirit. This would be hard to do as the Holy Spirit was fanning the flame inside of me. But I listened and continued to do what He said by sitting down in a quiet spot on my breaks reading the Word and minding my own business.

After about a week, my supervisor Ron made a comment to me about reading the Bible.

He said, "Is that a Bible You're reading?"

I said, "Yes" and smiled.

Then Ron told me, "That Bible stuff won't go over very well in this shop so it would be advised that you keep it to yourself."

I just nodded, smiled, acknowledged what he said and

stayed quiet. After Ron said that to me, I started to think about the culture that I was now a part of at this new job. It was different from the bowling alley culture that's for sure. The bowling alley fit my personality much better. It was more family structured and people were more social and friendly. Conversations were easy to strike up and it was a place that was easy to talk about the Bible because of the friendliness and comfortability there. Everybody got along with everybody, and there was hardly any confrontation.

The time I spent at the bowling alley allowed me to grow in the Lord. I spent eight years, from when I was saved in 1992 up until the year 2000, learning who I am in the Lord. I had the freedom to read His Word and meditate on the Scriptures daily. I was able to learn how to pray and develop a relationship with my Savior. I was able to receive the gift of tongues, among other gifts of the Spirit, and learn how to intercede for others right there in the back of the bowling alley. I learned how to listen to people talk before I would speak. And when I would speak, I learned to be led by the Holy Spirit about key points that are brought up in conversations- from those seeking answers, to the skeptics as well. Conversations about creationism vs evolution, other religions vs Christianity, evidence of the Resurrection, and so on.

Also at the bowling alley, I built up my confidence in the Lord and learned to rely on His Word. This would cause me to become stubborn in the Lord. No one can move me to think that God Almighty is not the true God of this world and the universe. No one can move me to think that Jesus never walked the earth, or the resurrection is not real. On the contrary, God Almighty, Yeshua, Elohim, is my God and Jesus Christ the only begotten Son died for my sin, and He alone is my Savior. He continued to fan the flame as I was gaining confidence in Him.

Fear Takes Root

But now, the foundation that was built is now being challenged by a culture that is more abrasive, rigid and very confrontational. Where people are more set in their ways, very stubborn, and hard to talk to about anything God related, let alone anything spiritual. It was a culture of arrogance and self-centered condescending conversations. Many of the conversations at this shop were about women. This angered me because of the verbal arrogance they would have, and they spoke like women are less than. They would talk about women like they were stupid or something. The swearing and cursing were nonstop all day long, and the conversations always had sexual content. This was an everyday occurrence from the time I punched in until the time I punched out. Something I was not used to at all, and it actually struck the fear of rejection in me.

Because I was non-confrontational and did not want to be rejected, I became very intimidated by my co-workers. I started to become timid in my spirit. I concluded that if I did say anything about God at all I would get cussed out and made fun of for my faith. Fear started to take root. I felt like a vulnerable target, and I was alone with no one to work with. When the Holy Spirit told me to sit quietly by myself and mind my own business and not draw any attention to myself, I was more than happy to do that. Being confrontational was something I was not sure about.

I started to think that maybe I made a wrong decision to take this job, and now everything was in question. I didn't want to go to work anymore, and the job became very stressful. Even though I felt like God wanted to set the place on fire with His Holy Spirit, I was now focused on the worldly culture within this shop. Fear and intimidation were where I camped out with my emotions and feelings. I allowed this fear of rejection to take root in me like a weed and it started to choke the Word of God out of me. I would just quietly read my Bible and try not to draw any attention to myself.

God Builds My Confidence – Vision #1

God Almighty started to do something about this fear of rejection and timidity that was developing. One day when I was praying inside the shop, and He gave me a vision. The shop had a section where the walls went up about 40 feet. While I was in a prayerful mindset I looked and about 30 feet up I saw a waterfall coming out of one of those walls and into the shop. My eyes were wide open but what I saw was in the spirit realm. Then I looked on the floor and I could see the waterfall going into a deep reservoir. It had to be an endless reservoir because the waterfall was a good size and as it went into the reservoir it never overflowed over the edge. But there was flowing water coming from the reservoir onto the shop floor about a quarter inch deep with water puddles as well.

Then the Holy Spirit allowed me to hear the waterfall. It was like the sound of a small waterfall, very peaceful and relaxing. Hearing the water was a reminder to me how gentle, yet powerful God Almighty is. And the puddles reminded me that the Holy Spirit was at the beginning of doing something in this shop. Something bigger than me. Like a kid I thought I would jump in the puddles. Silly I know but I think it's ok to be a kid in God's eyes.

I would see and hear this waterfall for several days and every day the water would fill the floor more and more. I could actually hear my feet stepping into the flowing water and into the puddles. Once in a while I would see splashes of water come from the top of the waterfall as if it was becoming restless and wanted to break loose. The water eventually came up to my ankles. I could really sense the presence of God Almighty in this shop every day. It was building my confidence more and more.

I heard the Lord clearly tell me this: *"I the Lord Almighty will do great things in this place through My Spirit."* I have definitely heard many voices throughout my life but this one was different. Seeing and hearing this waterfall, and now, hearing this voice speak in my spirit was amazing. I just remember feeling humbled, and grateful that God would involve me in something like this. I didn't know what to expect but my confidence in the Lord started to build up and become more established.

During this time, I had been doing a lot of reading in the book of Ezekiel. This vision the Lord had given me seemed really familiar. The Holy Spirit confirmed this vision in His Word in Ezekiel 47 *"Then he brought me back to the door of the temple, and behold, water was issuing from below the threshold of the temple toward the east (for the temple faced east). The water was flowing down from below the south end of the threshold of the temple, south of the altar. Then he brought me out by way of the north gate and led me around on the outside to the outer gate that faces toward the east; and behold, the water was trickling out on the south side. Going on eastward with a measuring line in his hand, the man measured a thousand cubits, and then led me through the water, and it was ankle-deep. Again he measured a thousand, and led me through the water, and it was knee-deep. Again he measured a thousand, and led me through the water, and it was waist-deep. Again he measured a thousand, and it was a river that I could not pass through, for the water had risen. It was deep enough to swim in, a river that could not be passed through. And he said to me, "Son of man, have you seen this?" Then he led me back to the bank of the river. As I went back, I saw on the bank of the river very many trees on the one side and on the other. And he said to me, "This water flows toward the eastern region and goes down into the Arabah, and enters the sea; when the water flows into the sea, the water will become fresh. And wherever the river goes, every living creature that swarms will live, and there will be very many fish. For this water goes there, that the waters of the sea may become fresh; so everything will live where the river goes. Fishermen will stand beside the sea. From Ein Gedi to En Eglaim it will be a place for the spreading of nets. Its fish will be of very many kinds, like the fish of the Great Sea. But it's swamps and marshes will not become fresh; they are to be left for salt. And on the banks, on* both sides of the river, there will grow all kinds of trees for food. Their leaves will not wither, nor their fruit fail, but they will bear fresh fruit every month, because the water for them flows from the sanctuary. Their fruit will be for food, and their leaves for healing."'* Ezekiel 47:1-12 ESV. After I read this passage of Scripture, I was consumed with the presence of God Almighty. He was confirming that these visions were from Him and that He was with me and ready to perform His Word.

The Water

The Holy Spirit started to clarify this vision in my spirit. As clear as day, the Holy Spirit told me that the water from the sanctuary is living water. Not stagnant or dirty, but rather fresh and satisfying - Living water! Just as the Scripture said in Ezekiel 47, this water will bring life to whoever touches it and turn salty water into fresh water. A fresh water that will bring life to those who are dead in their sin. A water where you will thirst no more just like the woman at the well. *"Jesus said to her, "Everyone who drinks of this water will be thirsty again, but whoever drinks of the water that I will give him will never be thirsty again. The water that I will give him will become in him a spring of water welling up to eternal life.""* John 4:13-14 ESV. I would see the workers of this shop walking in the streams of water, and I just simply believed that these people would be brought to Life as only the Holy Spirit can give. As I saw this, it was continuing to build my confidence.

Nets

The Holy Spirit confirmed in me that the nets being cast into the river will be the same as me casting nets to catch many fish as an evangelist. He kept telling me that I will be a fisher of men and there would be a great catch of many fish. The water being that of the Holy Spirit. *"And he said to them, "Follow me, and I will make you fishers of men.""* Matthew 4:19 ESV. The nets to me were the proclaiming of Christ Jesus. I heard in my heart to not be afraid of casting my nets all the time. I had a vision in prayer of me throwing the nets and catching fish on some casts and sometimes no fish. I saw myself casting many times. The Holy Spirit confirmed that I would be telling others about Christ Crucified and some will believe, and some will not believe. But I must not let rejection of the Gospel get to me and make me stop casting nets.

Tree and the Fruit

I was shown that I was to be like the tree who had its roots into the river of life. That I was to anchor myself into His Word and nothing else. That His Word would make the tree become strong and bear much fruit. *"but his delight is in the law of the Lord, and on his law he meditates day and night. He is like a tree planted by streams of water that yields its fruit in its season, and its leaf does not wither. In all that he does, he prospers."* Psalm 1:2-3 ESV. I was already in the habit of reading and meditating on God's Word. I believed that I would be like, as His Word says, a tree planted into the river of life. I would be able to withstand anything because of where I was rooted.

I saw in the Scriptures that Jesus and the Apostle Paul talked a lot about bearing fruit. Jesus makes it really simple *""Either make the tree good and its fruit good, or make the tree bad and its fruit bad, for the tree is known by its fruit."* Matthew 12:33 ESV. When I thought of that Scripture, I immediately thought of what Apostle Paul wrote in Galatians 5:22 *"But the fruit of the Spirit is love, joy, peace, patience, kindness, goodness, faithfulness, gentleness, self-control; against such things there is no law. And those who belong to Christ Jesus have crucified the flesh with its passions and desires."* Galatians 5:22 ESV.

After I realized that I needed to display the fruits of the Spirit I started to immediately pray that the Holy Spirit would help me and strengthen me to walk in the Spirit (Gal 5:16) so that I would not gratify the desires of the flesh. That I may walk in the fruits of the Holy Spirit as well. That He would make me into a tree that is rooted in the river of Life, that being the HolySpirit, I may bear fruit for His kingdom. To Him be the Glory! God Almighty again was building my confidence in Him and in Him alone.

A Mouthpiece?

As I am having Ezekiel 47 pressed into my spirit, the Holy Spirit took me to Ezekiel 33. I have read this chapter of the Bible several times but when I started reading this passage of Scripture this time it connected with my spirit. It was like I read it for the first time, and I didn't want to leave this chapter alone. I had to read it over and over, slowly so it would sink into my spirit. The verse that jumped out at me was *"The word of the Lord came to me: "Son of man, speak to your people and say to them, If I bring the sword upon a land, and the people of the land take a man from among them, and make him their watchman, and if he sees the sword coming upon the land and blows the trumpet and warns the people, then if anyone who hears the sound of the trumpet does not take warning, and the sword comes and takes him away, his blood shall be upon his own head. He heard the sound of the trumpet and did not take warning; his blood shall be upon himself. But if he had taken warning, he would have saved his life. But if the watchman sees the sword coming and does not blow the trumpet, so that the people are not warned, and the sword comes and takes any one of them, that person is taken away in his iniquity, but his blood I will require at the watchman's hand."* Ezekiel 33:1-6 ESV.

After letting that passage of Scripture sink in, the Holy Spirit spoke to me and said, *"You are to be a mouthpiece for the Lord and preach the Gospel to everyone in this shop."* I had to stop what I was doing to think about what I just heard in my spirit. This didn't sit well with me the first time I heard this. Then the Holy Spirit said to me again *"You are to be a mouthpiece for the Lord and preach the Gospel to everyone in this shop."* I set my Bible down to really give this some thought. I knew what the Holy Spirit was asking me; I just didn't want to accept it. I knew that preaching the Gospel was proclaiming Christ to the lost and hopeless. I was just in disbelief that it was being asked of me.

This was way out of my comfort zone. In my heart I wanted to see everyone saved and come to Christ. I wanted to be used in a way to be the one preaching the Word to the lost as well. I asked myself what the problem was? What was I so scared of? Well, I knew what I was scared of. I was in unfamiliar territory with a confrontational abrasive culture. I didn't want to take on these people that would reject the Gospel and make fun of me.

Sometimes you don't know what you are asking in prayer, you just know that your heart wants to proclaim Christ Jesus. That is where I was at with this. I was fearful of rejection so I explained to The Lord that "I can't do this because these men in this shop will resist everything that I say and will reject me and there will be confrontation. You know I can't handle that Lord".

The Holy Spirit would not give in to my initial reaction. He was gently persistent in letting me know what I was supposed to do at this shop, which was to preach the Gospel to everyone in that shop. I kept saying no and justifying it with lame excuses. I had what I'll call a Jonah complex. I really thought that the hearts of the people in this shop were too hard and would reject me. I didn't want the opposition of me preaching the Gospel to confront me. I imagined these co-workers getting in my face angrily and telling me to shut up and go home. I knew it wouldn't be like the culture I was used to. I wanted to get along with everyone and be everyone's friend like it was at the bowling alley the last 8 years. I was letting fear get the best of me and justify in my mind that I was the wrong guy for the job. I did not want to be rejected.

Obedience

As I continued to struggle, I kept reading Ezekiel 33 and the verse that kept resonating in my spirit was verse 6, " *But if the watchman sees the sword coming and does not blow the trumpet, so that the people are not warned, and the sword comes and takes any one of them, that person is taken away in his iniquity, but his blood I will require at the watchman's hand."* I just couldn't shake the fact that I was being called on to help these co-workers come to Christ. I continued to ask myself why I was so scared to do this. I mean I knew why, but I wouldn't have guessed that this fear of rejection would be so strong and make me resist what God Almighty is calling me to do.

With this conviction of what God Almighty is calling me to do, I decided to have a conversation with Him. I said to the Lord, "Is it my responsibility to warn them, Lord? To tell them to turn from their wicked ways and repent and turn to You?" In my spirit He said, "Yes." I thought, "Wait a minute, that is a serious Lord." He said "Yes, it is." Then I said, "So what you are telling me is that everyone You bring across my path who does not know You will be taken away by the sword if I do not warn them, and their blood is required of me?" He said, "Yes." I realized that God was entrusting me to share the Words of Life with all the people He brings my way in this shop who do not know Him. Then I said, "But Lord, when I speak Your Word what if they reject it and reject me?" Then the Lord reminded me of the last 4 verses in Ezekiel 33. ""*As for you, son of man, your people who talk together about you by the walls and at the doors of the houses, say to one another, each to his brother, 'Come, and hear what the word is that comes from the Lord.' And they come to you as people come, and they sit before you as my people, and they hear what you say but they will not do it; for with lustful talk in their mouths they act; their heart is set on their gain. And behold, you are to them like one who sings lustful songs with a beautiful voice and plays well on an instrument, for they hear what you say, but they will not do it. When this comes —and come it will!—then they will know that a prophet has been among them.""* Ezekiel 33:30-33 ESV. After reading that Scripture again, it finally took root into my heart. It was like a switch was hit and it all made sense. **No matter what, there will be people who will hear the Word of God, hear Christ Crucified, and still reject the Good News of Christ Jesus.**

I realized that proclaiming the Gospel and Christ Crucified had nothing to do with my feelings, but rather it is about being **obedient**. Allowing fear to settle in my spirit was keeping my mind distracted from focusing on the things above and preparing to preach the Gospel, as the Word of God commands us *"preach the word; be ready in season and out of season; reprove, rebuke, and exhort, with complete patience and teaching."* 2 Timothy 4:2 ESV. I struggled with making a commitment to be obedient, but I quickly settled in my heart that I will be obedient to be a mouthpiece for the sake of the Gospel and loudly proclaim Christ Crucified.

I realized that this is what I had been praying for a longtime. I asked God Almighty to open doors for me to preach the gospel and to use me to advance His kingdom. I prayed for the opportunity to lead a bible study and bring the Good News to the lost and dying. To bring hope to the hopeless. Here now, in this shop, is my opportunity. God Almighty heard my prayer and in His timing is now giving me a chance to step up and take on this calling to minister the Gospel.

CHAPTER 12
"The Word of God"

"I planted, Apollos watered, but God gave the growth." 1 Corinthians 3:6 ESV

Conversion?

As I settled in my heart to be a mouthpiece in this shop for the Lord Jesus, I still had more concerns to settle in my spirit. I started to think about my labor being in vain. I thought to myself, I may tell everyone about Jesus and give warning how sin separates us from God our Father (Isaiah 59:2), but my question was, how am I supposed to bring anyone to conversion? In my mind that was the goal of preaching the Gospel, to see unbelievers be saved. This was a genuine concern of mine.

The Holy Spirit, in His gentle way, gave me one of my most memorable moments with the Word of God. I was reading 1 Corinthians 3:6 *"I planted, Apollos watered, but God gave the growth."* 1 Corinthians 3:6 ESV. As I read that Scripture all I can say is those words came off the page. I'll never forget how that verse jumped out of my Bible and it was like I could see it in the spirit realm. I don't know how else to describe it. I just stared at this verse as it jumped out of my Bible. Then as clear as day I heard a voice say "Mike, conversion is not your concern. Preach the Gospel and I, the Lord, will make it grow." I felt anxiety lift off of me. I felt peace come over me and I started rejoicing in my spirit. It was like, now my mind was ready to take on the task that the Lord Almighty was calling me to do, preach the Gospel to everyone in this shop. There was such a freedom that came over me when this happened. It was like a door was closed on fear and rejection and the door was open to taking God at his Word.

I realized at that point that I was simply a laborer in a mission field of where the Lord has put me. In preaching the Gospel, my job was to be a sower of the Word of God. To tend to the fields of the ground he has given me. Now I understood my purpose for being at this shop. **My purpose is to sow the Word of God into the hearts of everyone in my sphere of influence. The plan is to pray, preach, and proclaim Christ Crucified. The vision is winning souls for the Lord's kingdom**. Now that I had this understanding of God's purpose, plan, and vision clearly, I was able to start getting my mind focused and prepared for the task at hand.

Plowman

The first thing that needed to happen was that I had to devote myself to prayer. Prayer is the foundation of proclaiming Christ Crucified to the people in any sphere of influence. When I started to pray for this calling to preach the Gospel at this shop, the Lord Jesus gave me another vision of a plowman. The plowman was dressed in what looked like a long one-piece robe with a hood that covered his head. Then the plowman showed me a plow, like from ancient Egyptians times. The tip of it was long and had extremely sharp edges. I knew in my spirit that this plow could till up the hardest of soils. I would actually see him put the plow tip into the hard soil and start to break it up. It was just the surface of the ground being tilled up, but it was a start to eventually making the ground soft and fertile.

The parable of the soils was brought to my spirit from the Holy Spirit. The Holy Spirit told me that, "The hearts of the people in this shop will be like the fallow ground, hard." This was the ground in the parable of the soils where the Word of God was sown, but because the ground was hard, and the birds came and snatched up the seed. *""Listen! Behold, a sower went out to sow. And as he sowed, some seed fell along the path, and the birds came and devoured it. And these are the ones along the path, where the word is sown: when they hear, Satan immediately comes and takes away the word that is sown in them."* Mark 4:3-4, 15 ESV

Then He told me this, "Praying will be the plow that will till up the soil of the fallow hearts of these people who need to hear the Gospel." This really excited me, and it all made sense. I was then prompted to start praying that this plow will be set down into the fallow ground of the hearts of everyone in this shop so that the seed of the Word of God could be planted in good soil. Every day I would pray that for my coworkers. I believed that the Holy Spirit was going before me and tilling up the soil and creating fertile ground. As I would pray this, the Holy Spirit would remind me of the Scripture 1 Corinthians 3:6 of how one plants, one waters, but God makes it grow.

Model For Preaching the Gospel

I was then led to read Colossians 4:2-6. *"Continue steadfastly in prayer, being watchful in it with thanksgiving. At the same time, pray also for us, that God may open to us a door for the word, to declare the mystery of Christ, on account of which I am in prison— that I may make it clear, which is how I ought to speak. Walk in wisdom toward outsiders, making the best use of the time. Let your speech always be gracious, seasoned with salt, so that you may know how you ought to answer each person."* Colossians 4:2-6 ESV.

This Scripture was the model to follow to effectively proclaim Christ Jesus to the sphere of influence that the Lord has given me. As I continued to ask the plowman to keep tilling up the fallow ground, I would also ask God Almighty for the opportunity to preach the gospel, which is sowing the seed. I couldn't just start walking up to people and say "Hey, you need Jesus, so repent and give your heart to Him." I had to believe that opportunities would come my way and the doors for preaching the gospel would be plentiful.

The next thing was to pray that the Word of God would manifest. Other versions of this verse use the word clearly instead of manifest - *"Pray that I may proclaim it clearly, as I should."* Colossians 4:4 NIV. Knowledge is one thing, and understanding is another. Anyone can obtain the knowledge by reading the Word or listening to it. This is why I would pray that the Word would be proclaimed clearly. In other words, the person listening to the Word would actually gain understanding of the knowledge they are obtaining. This would lead to people's hearts changing and them seeing that they need a Savior and turn from their sin.

Then I would pray that I would not lose my witness and believed God to protect my mind as I walked wisely among those around me. I knew I would sin. I did not want to display a loose attitude towards sin or be a slave to sin. I had to walk the walk – "If I was going to talk it, I had to walk it." I knew I would definitely come under a microscope and every move I made would be critically watched. I continued praying that I would use my time wisely to proclaim Christ Crucified.

Then lastly, I had to believe that the Holy Spirit would give me the right words to speak into the lives of the people around me. That I would only speak what He wanted me to speak. I really wanted my conversation to be filled with grace and bring life to those around me. I didn't want to contradict myself by speaking God's Word and proclaim Christ Crucified and then have gossip, cussing, and perversion come out of my mouth. **I had to believe that my conversations would be a blessing to those around me and bring a sense of peace.**

Every day I would also pray that the plowman would till up the fallow ground and the model of Colossians 4:2-6 would come to pass in my walk with the Lord Jesus. I was reminded by the Holy Spirit that it is important for me to remember that the hearts of those around me were hard like that of fallow ground. If I was to be an effective ambassador of the Gospel of Christ Jesus, then I would have to focus my prayer on the fallow ground, the hardened hearts of those around me. **Go before me and break up the fallow ground, Holy Spirit. May the words You give me to speak fall on fertile ground. Amen.** *"Sow for yourselves righteousness; reap steadfast love; break up your fallow ground, for it is the time to seek the Lord, that he may come and rain righteousness upon you."* Hosea 10:12 ESV.

Seeing the Deadman

One day at this shop there were five of us having a conversation. My supervisor, some machine builders, a pipefitter trainee, and myself. The conversation went to talking about women in a sexual way and they wanted me to join in on this conversation and agree with what they were saying about women. I wouldn't do that. During the whole time they were talking, Jesus opened my eyes to see them through His eyes. I saw something I will never forget. I could see within each one of them what I'll describe as a dead spirit being smothered by their depraved soul. They were dead in their sin *"And you were dead in the trespasses and sins"* Ephesians 2:1 ESV. Personally, I was once dead in my sin, but when I was saved, I was made alive in Christ Jesus (Ephesians 2:4-5).

When they were done with their conversation and laughing it up talking about fleshly desires there was such an emptiness in each one of them as they walked away and went about their day. Seeing their emptiness broke my heart. Instead of being offended about the things they were talking about I decided that I will continue to pray for them and ask God Almighty to til the ground of their hearts so the implanted Word can take root. I am so thankful that the Lord Almighty allowed me to see this because it was something that I was praying for, and it set the tone for what He was about to do. I was able to see people as God's creation who needed a Savior, not condemnation.

Prayer Driving to Work

As I drove to work, I would spend that time praying to my God, my Lord, my Savior. I continued to pray for the shop. I continued to pray that the plowman would till the hearts of everyone in that shop so when they hear the implanted Word of God it may take root. I prayed specifically that the Holy Spirit would remove the blinders, that they may see that the Lord is good, turn from their ways, and be saved. Then I asked the Lord to please give me the words to speak into the lives of the people around me. I also prayed that the Holy Spirit would overflow into the lives of those around me, and there would be a revival at this shop.

As I would pray this everyday there was a sense of boldness that was rising inside of me. I was becoming more confident to speak the Word of God to those around me. How could anyone know to put their faith in Christ Jesus unless someone tells them? How will anyone understand what salvation is, unless someone tells them? *"How then will they call on him in whom they have not believed? And how are they to believe in him of whom they have never heard? And how are they to hear without someone preaching? And how are they to preach unless they are sent? As it is written, "How beautiful are the feet of those who preach the good news!""* Romans 10:14-15 ESV.

I would watch co-workers as they interacted throughout the day, and this would help me understand more about their personality, which in turn would help me know what words to say to them. I would actually envision myself proclaiming Christ to these co-workers. I envisioned leading a Bible study at this shop. I would think about what I would say and if something wasn't flowing right, I would correct it and keep envisioning it. It was like I was practicing proclaiming Christ before I actually proclaimed Christ. I envisioned myself being bold and stepping out saying things to people as the Spirit would lead me. In doing this, a bold confidence was building, and fear continued dissipating.

Demons and the Word

I also started to gain more confidence in the arena of spiritual warfare prayer. The Holy Spirit would remind me that every person I saw in that shop was dealing with something. Things like grief, addiction, lust, divorce, suicide, and, simply put, people are hurting. I started to realize the intensity that there was a world out there who needed Jesus Christ as their Savior, their living hope. I started to see people as God's creation more defined and it was up to me to display the love of Christ to those who are in my sphere of influence. It was like these people around me were lost and blinded by the devil and his schemes, and the devil was doing everything he could to destroy the creation of God Almighty.

This made me so angry at the devil. I had a personal experience myself with the devil oppressing me and taking me to places of depression and trying to destroy me. This world of the devil offers nothing but heartache and disappointment. Negative thinking is like a cancer that cannot be cured. It makes you believe that you are gaining something but then it turns around and beats you down into a shameful spiral of self-destruction. This world system is not of God. This world system was created by the devil.

God was also showing me that each person is either a believer or unbeliever. There is nothing in between. You are either saved by grace or you are lost. I read too much Scripture to believe there is any gray area. It is either of God or it is of the devil. This is why the devil has worked hard at railing against God's Word and what has been taught since Adam and Eve. The devil has done nothing but wage war against God's people and blinded the lost to seeing the truth and being saved. He has been doing this since Adam and Eve. He deceived them by twisting the Word of God and now does the exact same thing to people today.

The devil is making war against God's creation, which is us. This Scripture hit me hard when I read, *"Then the dragon was enraged at the woman and went off to wage war against the rest of her offspring—those who keep God's commands and hold fast their testimony about Jesus."* Revelation 12:17 NIV. The dragon (Satan) is enraged (wanting to destroy) and is making war against God's people. When I read this, I got a vision of being chased by three dogs and eventually I was cornered with nowhere to go. If I did nothing, then the dogs won, and they would have no mercy towards me. Or, I could stand on the Word of God and speak truth of who those dogs really are. Remind them that they are already defeated by the death burial and resurrection of Christ Jesus. Which then would give me the victory because I'm standing on the Word of God.

With that in mind, the Holy Spirit showed me that if I do nothing, then Satan wins because he is making war against me, my family, and my friends. Or I could speak the Word of God, like I have been doing, and believe that what I say according to God's Word is truth. Because of the truth the dogs will become nothing and coward away. I was reminded of how I was oppressed by Satan most of my life. The dogs I faced were held back from devouring me only by the mercy of God the Father. Just as someone speaks to a dog in a voice of authority, that dog will listen and back off because the voice of authority has spoken. The Holy Spirit then told me that this is how I am to do spiritual warfare. Use the Word of God and speak it with authority.

I had to get it into my spirit that my victory and authority came from Christ Jesus and Him alone. *"But thanks be to God! He gives us the victory through our Lord Jesus Christ."* 1 Corinthians 15:57 NIV. We as believers have victory - Hallelujah. Satan was already defeated and so was death *"Since the children have flesh and blood, he too shared in their humanity so that by his death he might break the power of him who holds the power of death—that is, the devil— and free those who all their lives were held in slavery by their fear of death."* Hebrews 2:14-15 NIV.

It Is Written

To help me understand the power of the Word of God, the Holy Spirit then took me to the Scriptures in Matthew 4, *"Then Jesus was led up by the Spirit into the wilderness to be tempted by the devil. And after fasting forty days and forty nights, he was hungry. And the tempter came and said to him, "If you are the Son of God, command these stones to become loaves of bread." But he answered, "It is written, "'Man shall not live by bread alone, but by every word that comes from the mouth of God.'" Then the devil took him to the holy city and set him on the pinnacle of the temple and said to him, "If you are the Son of God, throw yourself down, for it is written, "'He will command his angels concerning you,' and "'On their hands they will bear you up, lest you strike your foot against a stone.'" Jesus said to him, "Again it is written, 'You shall not put the Lord your God to the test.'" Again, the devil took him to a very high mountain and showed him all the kingdoms of the world and their glory. And he said to him, "All these I will give you, if you will fall down and worship me." Then Jesus said to him, "Be gone, Satan! For it is written, "'You shall worship the Lord your God and him only shall you serve.'" Then the devil left him, and behold, angels came and were ministering to him."* Matthew 4:1-11 ESV.

As I read the account of Jesus being tempted in Matthew chapter 4, there were three words that stuck out to me: *it is written*. When Jesus said *it is written*, it means He is quoting something that was already written down somewhere. He is giving up any control, and He believed that what He was quoting was truth. It wasn't Jesus Himself resisting the temptations of Satan, it was His believing the Word of God to be the truth. Satan is a liar and what he says cannot stand up against the truth of the Word of God. Jesus quoted Scripture from the book of

Deuteronomy 8:3, 6:13, and 6:16. My thinking was that if Jesus thought it was a good idea to quote Scripture to resist the devil, then it must be a good idea for me to do the same.

Now, I had to train myself to believe the Word of God and learn to have a bold conviction. I figured if the devil could not stand against the truth of the Word of God, then no one could. I already knew that the devil was a liar and Jesus was the truth. Truth always wins because a lie has no foundation to stand on. I would ask that any lie within my soul that I believed would be revealed and then uprooted. God Almighty was always faithful to do this. This would lead to a time of drawing closer to Him and His Presence. As it became a habit, I would ask Him to show me my sin that I don't see and then ask Him to forgive me.

I also asked Him to allow the Word to become more real to me and that I would have more confidence in Him through His Word. When I would pray this way, the Holy Spirit would take me to Scriptures to pray. This was a Scripture I would pray over myself and personalize it: *"Let the word of Christ dwell in you richly, teaching and admonishing one another in all wisdom, singing psalms and hymns and spiritual songs, with thankfulness in your hearts to God. And whatever you do, in word or deed, do everything in the name of the Lord Jesus, giving thanks to God the Father through him."* Colossians 3:16-17 ESV. When I personalized it, this is how I would pray it over me: "Let the word of Christ dwell in me richly, teaching and admonishing me in all wisdom, as I sing psalms and hymns and spiritual songs, with a thankful heart to You God. Help me in whatever I do, in word, deed, and in everything in the name of the Lord Jesus, I give thanks to You my God and Father. Amen."

This was a new way to pray for myself. I had already been praying the Apostle Paul's prayers over myself, but now I was learning to take any Scripture and pray it over myself. After all, it was the Word of God. I could use any part of the Word of God to pray over myself. Then the light bulb went off and I realized that as I take the Word and pray it over myself, it is a form of spiritual warfare. When I prayed Scriptures, which I believed to be truth, the devil could not stand against it because he is a liar. Lies cannot stand against truth. Good versus evil. Truth versus lies.

The only way a liar can win is if he twists the truth to seem like a lie, and then makes that lie seem like the truth. Case in point is the story of Adam and Eve when they were deceived by the serpent. The serpent took what God Almighty told them would happen if they ate of the Tree of Knowledge and caused them to doubt what God told them. The Word was set in place for Adam and Eve to either believe it to be true or not. If we remember the serpent used this lie to create doubt, *"But the serpent said to the woman, "You will not surely die."* Genesis 3:4 ESV. The devil flat out lied to Eve and said, 'you won't die'. This was casting doubt about what God said to them and actually now made God look like the one who was the liar and the one who was repressing the idea that they could be like God. The serpent created doubt by lying to Adam and Eve and then caused them to not believe what the Word of God said.

I started to ask God Almighty to continue to let the Word dwell in me richly (Col 3:16) that I may have confidence in Him and trust Him, so I'll be like the tree rooting myself in the rivers of life (Jer 17:7-8). That He would be my salvation and my stronghold (Psalm 27:1) that He would see if there were any offensive ways in me and lead me in the way everlasting (Psalm 139:23-24). I would ask the Lord to cleanse me and purge me of my sin (Psalm 51:2,7) to help me stay fixed on Christ Jesus so I can run the race He has marked out for me (Heb 12:1-2). I was using the Word of God to pray, and it would be the beginning of me understanding how to do spiritual warfare prayer.

Armor of God

I set in my mind that I would be a front-line warrior for Christ Jesus. To suit up and put on the armor of God and to be strong in the Lord, standing against the schemes of the devil.

This passage of Scripture in Ephesians was pressed into my spirit of how I am supposed to stand in the truth of His Word and be used to proclaim Christ Crucified. *"Finally, be strong in the Lord and in the strength of his might. Put on the whole armor of God, that you may be able to stand against the schemes of the devil. For we do not wrestle against flesh and blood, but against the rulers, against the authorities, against the cosmic powers over this present darkness, against the spiritual forces of evil in the heavenly places. Therefore take up the whole armor of God, that you may be able to withstand in the evil day, and having done all, to stand firm. Stand therefore, having fastened on the belt of truth, and having put on the breastplate of righteousness, and, as shoes for your feet, having put on the readiness given by the gospel of peace. In all circumstances take up the shield of faith, with which you can extinguish all the flaming darts of the evil one; and take the helmet of salvation, and the sword of the Spirit, which is the word of God, praying at all times in the Spirit, with all prayer and supplication. To that end, keep alert with all perseverance, making supplication for all the saints, and also for me, that words may be given to me in opening my mouth boldly to proclaim the mystery of the gospel, for which I am an ambassador in chains, that I may declare it boldly, as I ought to speak."* Ephesians 6:10-20 ESV

The whole suit of armor that Paul is referring to has to do with the Word of God. The belt of truth, which is the Word of God. *"Sanctify them in the truth; your word is truth."* John 17:17 ESV. The breastplate of righteousness which is obedience to God's Word, *"Do you not know that if you present yourselves to anyone as obedient slaves, you are slaves of the one whom you obey, either of sin, which leads to death, or of obedience, which leads to righteousness?"* Romans 6:16 ESV. Obedience to the Word leads to righteousness. Feet with the readiness to preach the Word, *"And how are they to preach unless they are sent? As it is written, "How beautiful are the feet of those who preach the good news!""* Romans 10:15 ESV. Go and preach Christ Crucified. The shield of faith, faith in the Word of God. *"So faith comes from hearing, and hearing through the word of Christ."* Romans 10:17 ERSV. The helmet of salvation protects the mind from being polluted with the things of this world, *"Do not be conformed to this world, but be transformed by the renewal of your mind, that by testing you may discern what is the will of God, what is good and acceptable and perfect."* Romans 12:2 ESV. The only way to renew the mind is to read and believe the Word of God. And lastly, the Sword of the Spirit is the Word of God. The verse actually says that it is the Word. Here is another verse to go with that, *"For the word of God is living and active, sharper than any two-edged sword, piercing to the division of soul and of spirit, of joints and of marrow, and discerning the thoughts and intentions of the heart."* Hebrews 4:12 ESV.

This, again, was a huge revelation for me to understand from a different angle, that my walk with Christ Jesus was to be founded in the Word of God. Nothing else. No other doctrine or philosophy. No other religion. The Word of God and that is it. I wanted to be obedient to the Word of God and not allow the enemy to do anything to me or snatch anyone away from me. I made up my mind that I will solely believe the Word of God and take it at face value for what it says. I dug in deeper to memorize the Word and always had my Bible when praying. I would develop habits of praying in the Spirit and tried to have as much communion with God that I could.

While I was doing that, I was allowed an opportunity by the Holy Spirit to apply what I was learning on how the devil cannot stand against the Word of God. I was at Christi's house one night while she was at work, when there was an obvious presence in the room that was evil. I had my Bible open on the coffee table from some studying I was doing earlier. I sat back down on the couch and was just relaxing for a minute before I was going to start reading my Bible again. All of a sudden, I could feel this evil presence getting stronger. I physically felt something wrapping around me like a snake and before I knew it my body was paralyzed, and I could not speak. As I looked at my Bible, frozen and mute, within my mind, spirit, I heard the Holy Spirit tell me to start saying, "In the Name of Jesus" over and over. I did what the Holy Spirit told me to do and repeated "In the Name of Jesus" over and over in my mind. The next thing I knew my mouth was able to speak again and blurted out "In the name of Jesus" and then I felt this demon loosen its grip on me physically.

I immediately grabbed my Bible and started to quote Scripture. Psalm 91 to be exact. As my eyes were open to see this demon attacking me, I was able to speak the Word of God and cast it out. I then walked through the house and prayed and spoke the Word of God over the house and then Christi even though she was at work. There is power in the spoken Word. This was not done of any authority I had, but only the superior authority that Christ Jesus has over demons. I was just using the Word of God as my defense and my offense to protect what God has given me.

Praying the Armor for Others

But the biggest revelation as to how to wield the Sword of the Spirit was to do it in love. Anyone can fire off Scriptures. Even unbelievers can fire off Scriptures. But speaking the Word in love is the foundation of using the Sword of the Spirit. I understood that I couldn't just pick up the sword and start wielding it anywhere. I used to wield the Sword of the Spirit within my own strength, and it made me arrogant and hurt many people. I was being irresponsible. I did not want to go back to doing that, so I had to learn how to use the Sword of Spirit responsibly. I looked at it as training. Just like someone who wanted to learn sword fighting. I had to think about how to train myself up and wield the Sword of God's Word in love.

I would speak protection around my family everyday as if they were continually attacked. Attack meaning believing lies. The devil is the father of lies and a deceiver. I would speak over my family that the lies of the enemy would be destroyed and uprooted. That the mouth of the demons would be muzzled.

I would speak protection around the people I was given the opportunity to plant seeds of the Word of God. That they too would not believe the lies the enemy would spew on them, but instead they would adhere to the belt of truth. I would also speak that family, friends, and those I'm planting seed, would be protected by the shield of faith and extinguish all the flaming arrows of the evil one. Then I would ask that my mind would be protected from the world's ways by the helmet of salvation and that my sword would always be sharp and ready to cut to the hearts of people to repent and be saved. In Jesus Name, Amen!

CHAPTER 13
"Expectation"

"Then the Lord said to me, "You have seen well, for I am watching over my word to perform it."" Jeremiah 1:12 ESV

Proclaiming Christ Begins

One day at work, as I was praying under my breath and trying to not draw attention to myself, a new pipefitter walked over to see me.

He came up to me and said, "I see that you read your Bible."

Now I didn't know what to expect after he said that. I really thought he was going to confront me because of it.

I cautiously said to him, "Yes I do."

He put his arm on my shoulder and said, "Well, I think that is great. It's good to see another Christian brother in this shop."

Then he introduced himself, his name was Jeff. I was relieved to find out he was a Christian. We made some small talk, and I told Jeff about how I wanted to start a Bible study in that shop. I also shared my heart of how I wanted to see the lost saved and that Christ would be proclaimed.

The next thing I know, Jeff tells me that he rides with a guy who needs Jesus and was wondering what break the Bible study was. I reminded Jeff that I haven't started the Bible study yet and I was still praying about it, waiting on God's timing. But that didn't matter, Jeff was persistent to bring this guy over and hear the Word of God. After trying to get Jeff to wait on the

Bible study, he wouldn't take no for an answer. He told me that he would see me at the next break with this guy he rides with. I guess God's timing was *right now*.

My heart was pounding, and I had a slight freak out moment. I started to pray and ask God what just happened and what I should do the Bible study on. I was not prepared at all. The next thing I know the Holy Spirit calmed me down and reminded me that He has this. That He is the one orchestrating this and everything will be ok.

After I calmed down, I asked the Holy Spirit what I should read out of the Bible and what I should say. All I heard was Psalm 103. I had to question it because it wasn't what I expected. But nonetheless, I wanted to be obedient to what the Lord was telling me. I went and got my Bible and found Psalm 103 and read it to be prepared when Jeff and this guy came over to hear the Word of God. My prayer was, "Lord Jesus, help me have the words to speak and let Your name be glorified and I thank you for this opportunity."

I was wondering to myself why I was so nervous about doing this. I was used to sharing Christ from the stage when I was in Liquid Eclipse. I was preaching the Gospel to friends at the bowling alley. I did Bible studies with people I knew, and yet I was still nervous. Then it dawned on me. I was reminded how easy it was to proclaim Christ to them because there was a familiarity, and I was friends with them. I just met these guys - they are total strangers to me which, with my logic, would set the stage for confrontation. I didn't know what was going to happen. The Holy Spirit reminded me that He is with me, and He will do the work, which was encouraging. God had been preparing me for this moment.

It was getting close to breaktime and I was feeling a bit anxious. But I already prayed and was believing God Almighty to make a difference in both their hearts. Jeff and his friend made their way over and we introduced ourselves. The guy's name was Jason. To get the ball rolling, I opened with prayer and announced that I'll be reading in Psalm 103. As I was reading it,

THE SOWER

I got to the part that started to talk about God's amazing mercy and grace. His steadfast love, and how our sin is removed as far as the east is from the west. Then it made sense what God was doing. *"The Lord is compassionate and merciful, slow to get angry and filled with unfailing love. He will not constantly accuse us, nor remain angry forever. He does not punish us for all our sins; he does not deal harshly with us, as we deserve. For his unfailing love toward those who fear him is as great as the height of the heavens above the earth. He has removed our sins as far from us as the east is from the west."* Psalms 103:8-12 NLT. I didn't have a lot of time to expound on this Scripture, so I tried to make it concise and to the point. I talked about how our sin separates us from God, but if we believe in Him, we will be saved, and our sin is washed away. All this because He loves us.

As we ended the short Bible study I said to Jason, "Hey man, if you can remember anything about our Bible study today remember this: God loves you, Jesus died for you, and your sin is forgiven."

Jason had this 'thinking' look on his face, nodded his head, and went back to work. Jeff came up to me after Jason left and encouraged me on what a good job I did. Of course, it was the Lord Jesus that did it. I was just trying to say something that Jason would remember. But I appreciated the encouragement. This was the first time ever that I proclaimed Christ to someone I met for one minute and a total stranger.

The next day just before the first break Jeff found me to tell me that he had some good news. He went on to tell me that Jason was in one of the machines we were building, and he broke down and cried out to Jesus to forgive him of his sin. Jeff said that Jason is now saved in Christ Jesus Name. I was so overwhelmed with joy and set back by the amazing thing that God Almighty said He was going to do. This set me on fire. All fear was gone, and I set in my mind that this place really is going to have a Holy Spirit revival. I believed in my heart that God was executing His Word and that He was answering prayer. I was amazed and humbled and so looking forward to the days to come to see what else the Lord was going to do. I now had an expectation in my approach to each day as I would work there.

It Starts to Grow

Jason and Jeff start coming over on our breaks to hear the Word of God. I had to come up with a plan as to what we would study. As I prayed, I sensed in my spirit that the Holy Spirit wanted us to start going through the book of Matthew. I ended up bringing in some extra Bibles so Jason and Jeff would have something to follow along with when I read the Scripture for the day. I was so excited to have two people coming every day to be a part of the Bible study.

About a week went by, and the next thing I know there were two more people who came to join us. Jeff took it upon himself to invite others from the shop to come hear the Word of God. One was a Catholic and the other was a Baptist. Jeff came from a Pentecostal background and Jason had no church upbringing. This made an interesting group for sure. I would encourage everyone there to join in the conversation of what God was saying through His Word. I didn't want it to be me preaching, but rather, make it interactive. The Holy Spirit grew the Bible study up to four people now.

Then another guy joined us named Cliff. In the morning he would come over with his bowl of oatmeal and just listen to the Bible study. He would pull me aside and talk to me about his thoughts of what I was saying. Come to find out, he was a well-versed Baptist. Cliff liked listening to us, but he did have a difference of opinion on some things. Yet he decided to keep to himself because he didn't want to create any friction between us. His perspective was that he was glad I was leading a Bible study and could see there was already some fruit with people coming to it. He set aside his differences and said he would support me and pray for me and what God was doing. I was really impressed with Cliff. He had such a wealth of knowledge, and he eventually would share his thoughts but not become argumentative at all. He did keep me on my toes with his views of the Scriptures, which I thought was a great thing. Now we had five people in the Bible study.

Stop Doing It

Word started to spread through the shop that there was a Bible study going on and I was the one leading it. Because it was a Bible study, people started to say things to me. They would tell me they thought a Bible study was a terrible idea. They would make fun of me and laugh at me. They wanted me to stop doing the Bible study. I learned that all Satan can do is try and slow down what God has set into motion. The devil will try to convince you that you shouldn't do something for God through the words of other people. That's all he has. He is not stronger than God and he is not able to stop God. I would continue to remind myself how the devil is defeated and cannot stop what God has put into motion.

This gave me more motivation to dig in and keep it going. All of the verbal assaults did not affect me at all. Usually when someone would become verbally aggressive towards me I would back down and become timid. The Holy Spirit would always remind me that He is with me and there is nothing to be afraid of. *"Little children, you are from God and have overcome them, for he who is in you is greater than he who is in the world."* 1 John 4:4 ESV. Anyone who was cursing me, or the Bible study, I would make a point to pray for them. This allowed me to see them through the eyes of Jesus and keep focused on the task at hand- proclaiming Christ.

Those around me were always trying to trap me and get me to join in with the culture of that shop. They would go out of their way to try and cause me to openly sin. It would seem that almost every toolbox would have pictures of nude women. I was able to resist looking at the nude pictures they posted on their toolboxes and not let it affect me. One pipefitter was upset that I wouldn't look at the pictures on his toolbox, so he grabbed one of the nude pictures and chased me down the walkway with it. While he walked towards me with this nude picture, he was saying that one look wouldn't hurt. I would not give in and look.

One day, I was clamping a hydraulic pipe to some strut, and it wasn't going smooth. But I was patient and did not let it anger me and cause me to say something wrong. I took a deep breath to take a mental break from getting this hydraulic line to clamp down right. I stepped off the ladder, turned around, and there was this builder, Harry, staring at me.

I said, "Hey what's up Harry?"

He looked at me and said, "I'm just waiting for you to sin."

That comment threw me off a little. I smiled and explained to him that I am a sinner saved by grace and I am nothing without Christ in my life. He explained to me that there was something different about me and it perplexed him. I had an opportunity to clearly share the gospel with Harry that day. He did not give his heart to Jesus that day, but I am thankful I was able to plant the seed of the Gospel in his heart.

God Will Perform His Word

I knew I would be under the microscope while putting myself out there that I am a follower of Christ Jesus and leading a Bible study- it just comes with the territory. It was as if those opposed to the Bible study wanted to purposely tempt me to fall. They were expecting me to fall. I had to keep myself prayed up and focused on Christ Jesus. To do this, I changed my approach and attitude. As the Bible study was growing, I would have an expectation that my Lord, my God, would do something. Not in a material way, but rather in a Biblical way. I expected God to perform His word. *"Then the Lord said to me, "You have seen well, for I am watching over my word to perform it""* Jeremiah 1:12 ESV

I was being criticized by fellow Christian brothers and

sisters for having an expectation. Expectation was equated with telling my Sovereign God what to do. That was not the case. I was simply expecting Him to perform His Word. I expected Him to love without condemnation and know that no sin will keep Him from loving me or those around me. I expected Him to give mercy. Why? Because the Word of God says that He is a merciful God, therefore I should give others mercy as well. He is a God of Grace, and promised that it is a free gift from God for those who believe and are made alive in Christ. He promises to be near the broken-hearted and the downtrodden. He promises to give recovery of sight to the blind. He promises to set the captives free. I believed that my Lord, my Sovereign God, was going to do that in this shop. Why? Because it is who He is. God is love. I believed that I was being used to help pull his creation out of the darkness and into the light. These are the expectations I had of God, they are the promises of the Word of God. I knew that I could lean on the Word of God and His promises. This would help keep me going and stay focused on Christ Jesus to continue to minister the gospel in this shop. My expectation was simply believing God Almighty to perform His Word. I had an expectation that His promises are yes and amen, and I could count on them to be true.

Bench Talk

One day I was bending a tube, and this other pipefitter came up to the bench and started to talk about work related things. As a machine tool pipefitter, a part of our job is to bend steel tubing for air, hydraulics, and lube, and a lot of times we would bend the tube on what we call a bench. Sometimes there would be a wait to get on one of the benches, so of course conversations would be the normal. It was my turn to bend this tube on the bench. Then this fellow pipefitter looked me dead in the eye and asked me to tell him about Jesus. I was so excited that he asked me, and I couldn't believe that someone was point blank asking me about Jesus. I was jumping for joy inside myself.

I opened my mouth and started to tell him about the Bible and how awesome God is and all that He has done. I was quoting Scripture left and right giving him chapter and verse along with that. I was on a roll. I would look at him as I worked bending the tube, and he was just nodding away at all that I was saying. I thought to myself, this one is in the bag. It's going to be a slam dunk conversion here. I got done and looked at him expecting him to ask me how to be saved. I was thinking that I would pray with him, and he would be in the kingdom of God. Instead, he looked at me, thanked me for talking to him, then turned around and walked away.

I was actually shocked that he didn't give his heart to Jesus right there on the spot. I thought for sure that he would do that. I mean, I laid out the Bible with chapter and verse and told him all about Jesus. I was perplexed. Then something hit me, and I realized that I didn't proclaim Christ but instead I gave him a bunch of Bible knowledge. I did share the Gospel somewhere in that conversation, but it was masked over with me quoting Bible verses to him. I realized that I didn't give him a chance to talk, and all I did was listen to myself give him a 10-minute sermon on the Bible. I felt terrible about what I did and asked God to forgive me for blowing an opportunity and asked for the opportunity to talk to him again. I learned that I won't proclaim Christ correctly every time, and sometimes things like this happen. I asked God Almighty if there was any usable seed sown that would take root in this pipefitters' heart.

Junior

There was another pipefitter who struck a conversation with me about wanting to know Jesus. As he shared what was going on with him, I sensed he felt hopeless and wasn't happy with his lifestyle. I would listen to him talk about the emptiness he felt. He shared how when he drinks, he turns into a bad person. He told me that he does not want to drink anymore. He just wanted peace in his life. So I decided to proclaim Christ to him. After clearly explaining the Gospel to him, I felt in my spirit to explain to him that Christ Jesus is not like a magic wand to make problems go away. But Jesus does promise us that He will be there when we struggle and can give us peace in the midst of the storms of life. I emphasized that Jesus could take away his desire to drink and help keep his mind sober to think clearly.

He asked me what he would need to do to have Jesus in his life. I explained to him that he needs to repent and turn from his sin, confess Jesus is Lord and believe in his heart that He was raised from the dead, *"because, if you confess with your mouth that Jesus is Lord and believe in your heart that God raised him from the dead, you will be saved."* Romans 10:9 ESV.

He was still on the fence as to whether he wanted to know Jesus. I could tell the Holy Spirit was drawing him to God the Father. Junior then shared with me that his girlfriend was threatening to break up with him if he went to church. This was a tough one to try and counsel because she was a witch and didn't want anything to do with Jesus. In my spirit I really believed that the Holy Spirit wanted me to approach him with more sternness. I explained to him that as of right now they both are destined to hell and that witchcraft is an abomination to the Lord. Then I told him that to know Jesus, he would have to break up with her.

The next day he came and found me at a bench and told me that he broke up with his girlfriend and prayed and confessed Jesus as Lord believing He was raised from the dead. Hallelujah! I was so happy to hear that, and rejoiced with him that he was set free from being yoked with a witch and now Jesus is the Lord of his life. Then he told me he couldn't believe that his desire for drinking was gone as well. That was a glorious day for him and for me. The Lord did a great work in his life and set him free from the oppression he was under.

Entrusting

I recognized that the Lord was entrusting me with the souls of the people in this shop. This was a great responsibility because I was dealing with the inner spirit of the person. I could change the course of people's lives with what I said or with what I didn't say. There is tremendous power in the tongue. Like James said, it can be the spark to set a forest ablaze. Which means a word can tear someone down or build someone up. A word can paralyze someone emotionally or set them free. **A word can destroy someone's value, purpose, and worth, or build them up to conquer the world.** Just like in Scripture and proclaiming Christ, I can either speak arrogance and listen to what a good speaker I am, or humble myself and speak the words given by the Holy Spirit.

The Holy Spirit helped me have knowledge of the Scriptures and be able to memorize them. I learned that listening first is more important. How will I know what to say if I do not listen to what the person is saying? I had to learn the stories of the people in that shop before I could have something meaningful to say to them. The ones I proclaimed Christ too before I came to this shop, I knew their story, well at least some of their story, so there was a history already there. Luke, I knew since elementary schoool. I knew how to approach him at Landmark Lanes. The people I talked to during the Liquid Eclipse season were easier because it was a group setting. And those who came to see us perform were there because they wanted to be a part of a Christian event. But being in this shop, where people want nothing to do with Jesus, I had to learn to be patient and listen. Hear what their stories were, find out where they were coming from, and let them know that I care about what was going on in their lives. The saying is true that **people want to know that you care before they want to know what you know.**

Skeptics

There were many skeptics in that shop. There were two pipefitters in particular who made it a point to mock me and make fun of me when they would see me throughout the day. I was able to see them mocking me out of ignorance. In knowing that, it would make it easy to give them mercy and grace. But there was one other skeptic who made it his mission to always rail against what the Holy Spirit was trying to do there. He was a Psychology major and tried to explain to me that Christianity was a fallacy and Jesus was a myth. He would try and argue this with me all the time. My faith was not moved by what he said, but I found it interesting to debate with this co-worker. He would bring every angle he could think of against the Bible and Christ Jesus' death, burial, and resurrection.

I thought how a guy like this could lead many astray, because when he talked it was very convincing since he seemed to know what he was talking about. This was very alarming to me because he could snatch people up by giving them his arguments against God Almighty's existence. But for now, he seemed to be focused on me and not anyone else around him. I ended up having to work with the guy for a few weeks, so every day he wanted to debate the Scriptures. Now I am no debater, but I did know enough to hold my ground. I frustrated him because I would tell him it didn't matter what he said he could not shake my faith in Christ Jesus and what He did for me at the cross of Calvary.

Bible Study Keeps Growing

The Bible study continued to grow. There were now 10-12 people coming to it. I ended up putting together topics we could study for the week. On my computer at home, I would put together the outlines with the Scripture readings and then print them out. Then I would spend time putting them into packets for those who showed up to the Bible study. That way we were all on the same page and everyone knew what was going to be studied for the week. Proclaiming Christ was my priority at this shop, and every day there would be a Bible study at all three breaks. On top of that, every day in between the breaks I would talk to someone about the Bible or who Christ Jesus is. It was such an amazing time in my life.

The responsibility of leading this Bible study and proclaiming Christ Jesus started to wear me down. I found myself becoming really tired by midweek, and then by the weekends, I was exhausted. My work schedule was 58 hours a week, plus church on Sunday. When I would get home from church on Sunday, as a family we would all take a nap for the afternoon.

I realized that I needed to pay attention to the physical work I was doing and make sure I got good sleep. I also had to deflect stress. Doing those two things made a huge difference in keeping me going. I had to do things in the practical to help keep my focus on the spiritual. The Bible says to fix our eyes on the Author and Protector of our faith so we can run the race that is marked out for us (Heb 12:2). I realized really quickly that if I am physically worn down, I would start to waiver and lose momentum with what the Lord was doing.

My wife was a huge help in relieving stress in the practical. She took over printing out the Bible study outlines. She made sure there was no stress in our home when I would came home from work so I could wind my mind down. She made sure we were eating well and would remind me to get to bed so I wouldn't lose any sleep. She was helping make sure I was not overdoing my schedule. Even though I was really busy with church commitments, she made sure it didn't put me into an overload. She really stepped up and helped me out to make sure what I was doing at work was being effective and purposeful.

Community Prayer List

The Lord put on my heart to take a step of faith and believe that God Almighty would answer prayers for the people I worked with. I started a prayer list for anyone in the shop who wanted prayer for any type of prayer request. People would ask for prayer for their family members to be healed or for marriages to get better. For addictions to be broken and for peace of mind and so forth and so on. We started to see results among the Bible study group. These answered prayer results would spread around the whole shop. Those who were unbelievers and skeptics could not deny that God Almighty was answering prayer. And those who were mocking me and making fun of me for being a Jesus freak had to take note of what God Almighty was doing.

Then one day Harry the builder asked someone else to come get me because he had to talk to me. I thought it was kind of strange that Harry himself didn't come get me, but nonetheless, I went to his toolbox to talk to him. Harry very nervously said that he doesn't believe in Jesus and all but was wondering if I could put his wife on my prayer list because she had pneumonia and wasn't handling it very well. I said to Harry no problem and I'll start praying for her today.

The next few days went by, and two other skeptics each talked to me privately for prayer. One asked if I could pray for his marriage and even asked what the Bible says about marriage. The other asked for prayer for his marriage as well, and asked to pray that God helps him not drink so much. I was more than happy to pray for everyone including these two and give them what understanding I can from the Scriptures. They once mocked me and made fun of me, but now, they are asking for prayer and advice. Praise the Lord.

About a week went by and Harry called me over his toolbox to tell me that his wife had pulled through her pneumonia and will make a full recovery. Now, I already shared the gospel with Harry, but I took the opportunity to give God the Glory and remind Harry that Christ Jesus loves him and wants him to be saved and come to a knowledge of the truth. He was very receptive and said he would start going to church and give God more attention. Seed planting. I had to remind myself that I am a sower of the Word of God.

About the same time, one of the skeptics told me that his marriage is doing great and that what we prayed for, God answered. Again, give God the Glory. He said he was definitely going back to church and would get involved. Seed planting. The other skeptic was still having problems with his wife, and they ended up separating and I am not sure what happened after that. Hopefully they stayed together and worked it out. He thanked me for caring enough to talk to him and pray for him.

I was making myself available physically and emotionally. I was trying to make myself available to look at the needs of the co-workers in the shop. I was trying to be a sower of the Word of God with Bible study. I would continue praying for hearts to be tilled up and ready to speak life as the Holy Spirit leads. Praying for the needs of those whether they were saved or not. God was on the move and wasn't going to be stopped.

CHAPTER 14
"Love, Mercy, Grace"

"But God, being rich in mercy, because of the great love with which he loved us, even when we were dead in our trespasses, made us alive together with Christ—by grace you have been saved—" Ephesians 2:4-5 ESV

The Bible study was growing so fast that we had to continue to find bigger areas so everyone could sit down. I was doing the Bible study inside the shop instead of in a break room. This made it easier for everyone to show up. Some of those attending would sit a ways away and listen, so I found myself having to talk loudly to make sure they would hear the Word of God. I was printing out 20 packets of the lesson for the week to hand out on Monday for everyone to know what we would be going over for the week. It was amazing to see God Almighty grow this Bible study from one person to around twenty in about four months.

There were already people being saved, and the power of God was very evident. This is what God promised He would do. He told me to plant the Word of God and the Holy Spirit would make it grow. He told me to not worry about the conversions and He took care of that. His Word said to pray for the opportunity to proclaim Christ, and that the seed planted would take root. He had given ample opportunity with seeds of the Word taking root. He was continuing to show Himself as the All Powerful God His Word says He is. He showed me to pray and not be afraid of the enemy and He was continuing to protect me and my family and answering the prayers lifted up in His Name. It was amazing what My Savior was doing in that shop!

The fire of the Holy Spirit was continuing to spread throughout this shop. There was not one person who worked there who didn't know about the Bible study. The fruits of the Bible study and prayer were also being made known. There was no denying that Jehovah-Shammah was present and doing something. Those who warned me in the beginning about not doing the Bible study were now speaking well of it. They would say things like this, "I know I was against you doing a Bible study and I myself am just not into the God thing, but I think it's great that you are doing the Bible study." It was noted by supervisors that "People seemed to be happy and in a better mood." Of course, they were in a good mood, Jesus and the Holy Spirit were making things happen.

It became difficult to pray with everyone at the shop. I would be quite overwhelmed at times. I ended up writing down prayers for them to pray when they were alone. Most of the prayers I gave to people were for forgiveness, to repent and confess Jesus as Lord. And people would actually pray that prayer I wrote down for them and then come back and tell me they are now saved. Amazing. Others would tuck the prayer away for when they were ready. The goto prayer I would give people, if it wasn't a prayer of repentance, was Colossians 1:9-14, *"And so, from the day we heard, we have not ceased to pray for you, asking that you may be filled with the knowledge of his will in all spiritual wisdom and understanding, so as to walk in a manner worthy of the Lord, fully pleasing to him: bearing fruit in every good work and increasing in the knowledge of God; being strengthened with all power, according to his glorious might, for all endurance and patience with joy; giving thanks to the Father, who has qualified you to share in the inheritance of the saints in light. He has delivered us from the domain of darkness and transferred us to the kingdom of his beloved Son, in whom we have redemption, the forgiveness of sins."* Colossians 1:9-14 ESV. I eventually made copies of that prayer and kept them in my area to hand out when someone needed a copy to take home.

My fellow co-worker Josh, the one I surly thought would give his heart to Jesus on the spot after I laid out the gospel, kept the prayer I wrote down for him in his wallet. He told me when he is ready, he will pray that prayer. I wanted to help him through that prayer, but I had to trust the Holy Spirit to remind him to repent and ask for forgiveness. Or just believe that I was sowing seed for some else to receive the harvest.

People would come into that shop to work and then they could be gone in a month, whether it was because they were fired or just went to a different shop. That was the nature of being a contract pipefitter. I felt I had to give them something so they wouldn't forget what to pray. Several people would ask me how they should pray to God and ask Him to forgive them. Only a few would pray with me on the spot, but it didn't matter, because I was just trying to make sure everyone knew what to do when the time came for them to pray, ask God Almighty to forgive them, cleanse them, turn from their sin and repent.

As I was encouraged by the Lord, I was continually reminded of the vision He gave me to have the confidence to lead what He was doing there. I kept seeing the water rise more and more as the Bible Study grew and salvations were manifesting, and prayer was being answered. Glory to God. As I saw the waters continue to rise, I knew in my heart that I had to keep this going. When I prayed, I believed that God Almighty would give me strength, guidance, discernment, and continued boldness to proclaim Christ Crucified. I would pray that as a fisher of men I would cast my nets into the waters, and many would come to salvation.

By this time, I was able to gain the respect of everyone in the shop and they did not make fun of me anymore or mock me. The Lord was bearing fruit in my life just like the Scriptures said and my leaves were always green for healing. Within my spirit I was always trying to keep it simple and focus on proclaiming the good news of Christ Jesus. God was definitely doing what He said would happen and performing His Word. As I continued to follow the leading of the Holy Spirit, people were hearing the Word and gaining faith unto salvation. I am so thankful that I could be a part of what the Lord my God was doing.

Jimmy Wright

Along the way I developed awesome friendships. Jeff was a huge help all along the way of that journey. He was the guy who gathered everyone and invited everyone to come hear the Word of God. He also would keep me in prayer all the time. Which is something I coveted. Cliff and I became good friends, and both had tremendous respect for each other. He was the guy who kept me balanced by bringing into the Bible study his own perspective.

But there was another coworker who started coming to the Bible study named Jimmy Wright. Jimmy was an intimidating looking guy. Long hair, tattoos, and built solid. But he was not afraid to ask questions about the Bible. We spent a lot of time together while we worked talking about Scriptures and the things of God. He had such a desire to know God Almighty like a little kid exploring the world. He was the type who would ask the why to everything you tell him. Such a wonderful example of faith and desire to want to know God and His Word.

I had just finished doing a weeklong study on the gifts of the Holy Spirit in 1 Corinthians 12:4-11, and tongues are always the gift that Christians want to focus on receiving. He wanted to talk to me about the gift of tongues. He wanted more proof of what the Bible says about tongues. Let's face it, this is a strange concept to think that all of a sudden one could just speak in a language they have no idea what it is. Jimmy respected the Word of God. At this time in his life, he was a cautious Christian.

I took him to the book of Acts and showed him what happened after the day of Pentecost where the disciples were speaking in tongues and received the Holy Spirit.
We would talk about the purpose of tongues and what the Bible

said about it. This would become a daily conversation outside of the Bible studies.

I wanted him to see that tongues are the evidence of the Holy Spirit. There is a teaching that says one can lay hands on a believer and baptize them in the name of the Father, the Son, and the Holy Spirit and they will receive the gift of the Holy Spirit with the evidence of speaking in tongues. *"And it happened that while Apollos was at Corinth, Paul passed through the inland country and came to Ephesus. There he found some disciples. And he said to them, "Did you receive the Holy Spirit when you believed?" And they said, "No, we have not even heard that there is a Holy Spirit." And he said, "Into what then were you baptized?" They said, "Into John's baptism." And Paul said, "John baptized with the baptism of repentance, telling the people to believe in the one who was to come after him, that is, Jesus." On hearing this, they were baptized in the name of the Lord Jesus. And when Paul had laid his hands on them, the Holy Spirit came on them, and they began speaking in tongues and prophesying. There were about twelve men in all."* Acts 19:1-7 ESV.

I explained to Jimmy that there was a difference between the baptism of water and the baptism of the Holy Spirit. I tried to get him to understand that when he was baptized with water it was onto repentance just like the Apostle Paul says in this Scripture. Now there is the baptism of the Holy Spirit as Paul laid hands on these men and they spoke in tongues and prophesied. Jimmy made it clear to me that he wanted the gift of tongues and asked me to pray with him to receive it. I never had anyone ask me to lay hands on them and pray that they receive the Gift of the Holy Spirit with the evidence of tongues. I had no idea what to pray.

What I did was encourage Jimmy to learn more about what it means to walk in the Spirit of God and not gratify the desires of the flesh. This would mean going on a journey of studying His Word and getting to know the giver of the gift rather than the gift. Jimmy was a newborn Christian and was simply wanting more of God the Father. There is nothing wrong with that at all. We would continue to have what we called 'spiritual conversations' every day for several days. I saw his faith grow and the desires of the world become less desirable in his life. He still had things to work through, but who doesn't. He was a new creation after God's heart.

Then the day came for us to pray together for the gift of tongues. I ended up going over to his house one night and we prayed, and I laid hands on him. When we were done Jimmy did not receive tongues immediately but a few days after he was able to trust what the Holy Spirit was doing inside his belly and tongue, he started speaking in tongues. Praise the Lord. I emphasized with Jimmy to seek the greater gifts of the Holy Spirit like prophesying, but use the gift of tongues to recharge his spirit and pray for others when he didn't know what to pray.

Things Start to End

The Bible study started to dwindle away. The events of September 11th 2001 really hurt my job field as a contract pipefitter. Co-workers were either transferring to other shops or they were being laid-off. I found myself saying a lot of goodbyes to those who showed up to the Bible study consistently, or those who are now saved, because of what God Almighty did in that shop. It was a weekly event. Every Friday more co-workers would be saying goodbye. I tried to stay in touch with them after they left. We would exchange numbers and I let everyone know where they could find me. In other words, show up to a church service at the church I was attending at the time.

Then we got word that our shop was going to close. They had one more job to do for Chrysler then they were done. I was one of the chosen pipefitters to stay there and be on the last job of that shop. I was very thankful for this. God is good and always provides. I really didn't know if God was done in that shop or not. All my Bible study helpers were laid-off, and there were no other Christians in the shop to encourage one another. I was by myself. But I had such a peace when I was there, and I just had a feeling that God wasn't done.

Brady

The lead supervisor gave me a challenge to figure out. We would build pipe headers out of what they would call Tube Max. This was a special kind of pipe that would move hydraulic fluid. Usually, it would be in straight runs with fittings to make 90 degree turns. They bought a Tube Max bender to bend it at 90-degrees, but it wasn't quite working right. It was crushing the 90-degree bend and cracking the pipe. They gave me the responsibility to figure it out and make it bend the Tube Max correctly and have nice 90-degree bends. I tried to figure this out, but with no success.

An electrician mentioned that maybe I could bend the Tube Max on their conduit bender. I thought why not, what I'm doing isn't working. I grabbed some tube max and put it in the conduit bender and wouldn't you know it, it worked. I now had to figure out how to do the math correctly so the distances from bend to bend would be what I wanted. To do this I would need someone to help me because this tube max was heavy tubing.

The supervisor gave me one of the more experienced pipefitters to help me, his name was Brady. I thought this was a good idea because Brady was one pipefitter who wanted nothing to do with God, the Bible, or Jesus. I hadn't talked to him in a long time or even seen him. I think he had just come back to the shop after doing some install work out of state.

I pressed in my spirit to be very intentional to pray for him. I could really sense the oppression in his life blinding him from the truth. I prayed that there would be an opportunity to minister the Gospel of Christ Jesus to him. I also prayed that his eyes would see the truth of the gospel and that truth would set him free. He had anger issues, so I prayed that all his pain and anger would not hinder him from hearing the Gospel. Lastly, I prayed that the plowman continues to till the soil of his heart so the implanted Word of God would take root. I really believed our Sovereign God put him and I together for the purpose of hearing the Gospel and obtaining the faith to salvation.

Brady knew exactly what I was about and how I was the one leading the Bible study, and because of that he had some questions. He approached me one day when we were working together and said he wanted to know more about the Bible and church. I thought he was kidding because he was one who made it very clear that the Bible study was a waste of time and wanted nothing to do with God. He was one of the most abrasive and verbally abusive ones towards me. Because of this I was very hesitant that he may be leading me down a rabbit trail again only to set me up and mock me and make fun of me. I kept telling him that I will answer these questions when I know he is serious. He did take some offense to me telling him that.

Brady looked at me and said, "Mike, I am serious, I want to know what you know about God and church."

I finally realized that he was serious and started giving him my full attention. The first question he asked me was, "Tell me about God? Who is God?" What came to my mind at first to share with him was that God is love. *"Beloved, let us love one another, for love is from God, and whoever loves has been born of God and knows God. Anyone who does not love does not know God, because God is love."* 1 John 4:7-8 ESV. I expounded on the idea that in the Garden of Eden there was an amazing connection and relationship with God. How He created us for fellowship and to have a relationship with Him. Then I went to Psalm 103 and explained how God is gracious and merciful because of His great love for us. *"The Lord is merciful and gracious, slow to anger and abounding in steadfast love."* Psalm 103:8 ESV.

Every day that we worked together he would ask questions about the stories he knew from the Bible. Questions like if the story of Moses was for real, and if the flood actually happened. Then he started asking questions about the church and the traditions and sacraments of today. He was brought up in the church and had a tremendous amount of baggage from the church and his family situation. After talking with him more, he opened up and shared that he was adopted, and had a lot of trauma growing up and the church hurt him as well. Once he started to share these things, I had a better understanding of how to share the Good News of Jesus with him when the opportunity would arise.

It wasn't too long after he shared that with me that he started to ask specific questions about Christ Jesus. Even more specifically, how could he be forgiven of any of his past sins. He shared how he hurt so many people and let so many people down. He really had a tremendous burden of guilt and shame for all that he had done. I had to be patient and let him talk it through for a few days. I did tell Brady that because God is love, abounding grace and mercy was given to him through the blood of Jesus. I did encourage him that God is not holding his sin against him but rather is reaching out to him with compassion. Brady had a hard time accepting this.

The day did come where Brady asked me to explain to him how he could know Christ Jesus. This was answered prayer. The plowman had been working hard to soften the soil and till up the fallow ground of Brady's heart. I started from the beginning to help him understand that he has a sinful nature that has separated him from God the Father. That doesn't mean that he himself is a bad person, but rather the sinful nature is what keeps him from knowing Jesus, because God the Father and sin do not coexist. Sin is obliterated if it comes into the presence of God Almighty. Because He is a Holy God, and sin has no chance in His presence.

I explained it to Brady this way. Imagine there is a spacecraft heading towards the sun. The sun is 27 million degrees Fahrenheit. Now the sun cannot change what it is and become a comfortable temperature for the spacecraft to head into. The essence of the sun is 27 million degrees, it cannot help it or change itself. With that said, the spacecraft would disintegrate at some point and be obliterated. That's how it is with our sinful nature. As it tries to coexist in the Presence of our Holy God, it will disintegrate. And it is because of this that we are separated from God our Creator.

Then I went on to tell Brady this is why Jesus the Son of God had to come and save us from our sin. Because God so loved the world, He sent His only Son into the world that whoever believes in Him will have eternal life. "*"For God so loved the world, that he gave his only Son, that whoever believes in him should not perish but have eternal life."* John 3:16 ESV. Brady gave that look like the wheels were turning in his mind. Then I went on to tell him about the death, burial, and resurrection of Jesus, and how His blood sacrifice has taken away the sin of the world. That his sin is washed away in the blood of Jesus and because of that, he is now reconciled back to the Father. This made sense to Brady. I could tell he was getting what the Holy Spirit was telling him. But he was having a hard time believing that God the Father actually loved him without conditions.

He shared with me that he needed change. That he needed something different than what was going on in his life. He was tired of being drunk all the time and dealing with rejection issues on a daily basis. He asked me how God could forgive him of all his wrongdoing and how God could love him, a drunk and bitter person. I realized that he already recognized that he has a sinful nature and needed a Savior; he just couldn't believe that God the Father wanted him in His kingdom. I shared my testimony of how I struggled with God actually loving me and asked myself how could God Almighty even want me at all. I shared every Scripture I could think of to show through the Word of God that the Lord our God does in fact love him without condition. This would go on for about a week. Through this whole time, I could feel the presence of the Holy Spirit burning within me every time Brady and I would talk.

Then one day he surprised me and asked what he needed to do to have Jesus in his heart. I was so excited that Brady was ready to have Jesus the Lord of his life. I told him I wanted to ask him a few questions. I asked him if he understood that he was separated from our Heavenly Father because of his sin more specifically his sinful nature. He said yes. I asked him if he understood that Jesus came and died on a cross for his sin, was buried, and was risen on the third day. He said yes. I asked him if he could believe that Christ Jesus is the Lord of his life. He said yes. Then I asked him if he believed that Christ Jesus was the Son of God. He said yes.

I didn't really know exactly what to pray but I did know he was ready to make Christ Jesus Lord of his life. I asked him to simply ask Christ Jesus to forgive him, to wash away his sin, to cleanse him, to fill him with His Holy Spirit, and to reconcile him to Christ Jesus and thank Him for making him a new creation. I helped him through that prayer and Brady was saved that day. He asked me if that was it, I told him that is it. He was filled with joy and peace like no other after that day.

After the initial excitement of being saved, Brady asked me what he should do next. I told him to go to church and invited him to the church I was attending at the time. In the meantime, I now had the privilege of mentoring Brady as a new convert. I wanted to make sure I was watering the seed of the Word which led to salvation. I bought him a Bible and I ended up doing private Bible studies so he could start to understand who God Almighty is and of His steadfast love for us. Brady and I would study the Word together on our breaks.

One day he shared something with me that I will never forget. He wanted to thank me for not judging him or criticizing him for his worldly habits while he was asking questions and wanting to know more about Christ Jesus and the Bible. Before Brady was saved, he would still drink heavily during the day. I could smell the alcohol on his breath after lunch every day and his cussing would at times be too much where I had to go for a walk around the shop to clear my head. I mean, who am I to judge him and throw stones at him when I was doing the same thing when Regine was proclaiming Christ Jesus to me. There is no way I would push Brady away because of his sin. I saw Brady through the eyes of Jesus and prayed that I would have the patience to share the Gospel with him. But praise the Lord he gave up drinking cold turkey and didn't swear any more. I could believe it because it happened to me when I was saved as well. He was a new man with a new mind in Christ.

He went on to tell me more and said this: **because of the action of Christ's love being displayed through me he was able to trust me and listen to what I had to say because I did not judge him for his sin or reject him and make him feel worthless and ashamed.** Slow to speak and quick to listen. Looking past Brady's sin and being merciful and forgiving him had to happen for him to hear the Gospel. Remember this: **Nobody will listen to an arrogant, haughty person who is pointing out what a sinner they are.** Not at all. Be merciful as the Father in Heaven is merciful. He was merciful to me in my ignorance, so I am to do the same and be merciful. *"Then Peter came up and said to him, "Lord, how often will my brother sin against me, and I forgive him? As many as seven times?" Jesus said to him, "I do not say to you seven times, but seventy-seven times. "Therefore the kingdom of heaven may be compared to a king who wished to settle accounts with his servants. When he began to settle, one was brought to him who owed him ten thousand talents. And since he could not pay, his master ordered him to be sold, with his wife and children and all that he had, and payment to be made. So the servant fell on his knees, imploring him, 'Have patience with me, and I will pay you everything.' And out of pity for him, the master of that servant released him and forgave him the debt. But when that same servant went out, he found one of his fellow servants who owed him a hundred denarii, and seizing him, he began to choke him, saying, 'Pay what you owe.' So his fellow servant fell down and pleaded with him, 'Have patience with me, and I will pay you.' He refused and went and put him in prison until he should pay the debt. When his fellow servants saw what had taken place, they were greatly distressed, and they went and reported to their master all that had taken place. Then his master summoned him and said to him, 'You wicked servant! I forgave you all that debt because you pleaded with me. And should not you have had mercy on your fellow servant, as*

I had mercy on you?' And in anger his master delivered him to the jailers, until he should pay all his debt. So also my heavenly Father will do to every one of you, if you do not forgive your brother from your heart."' Matthew 18:21-35.

This would be a revelation that cut my heart and I gave him a hug and told him because God loved me and gave me mercy, I have to extend that same love and mercy to those around me. I had to be patient and realize that those around me who have offensive habitual sin do it out of ignorance. They sin because that is what they know. Also, who am I to say anything because I am still a sinner who is saved by the love of God the Father and His mercy which then gives us the free gift of grace.

Brady confirmed what I learned a while ago: **actions do speak louder than words, but actions also empower your words. The action of love, which is acceptance, is what Brady needed to create a foundation for him to hear the Gospel clearly and then the Holy Spirit could draw him to the Father through the implanted word of God.**

It Had to End

This would end an amazing journey that my Sovereign God would take me on to bring the Gospel of Christ Jesus to everyone in that shop. What an experience that was. I really did nothing except be obedient to do what God told me to do. I was obedient to say the things that the Holy Spirit told me to say. There was no magic formula or anything within myself that made things happen while I was there. It was solely the Holy Spirit. I was a sower of the Word of God into all of their lives, saved or not saved. Believer or unbeliever. The questioner or the skeptic. The timid or the aggressor. The mocker or the supporter. The spiritual or the logical. Everyone heard the Gospel, and everyone had a chance to repent and turn from their sin and be saved.

The growth was truly not up to me, but rather the work of the Holy Spirit. I was just the laborer in the fields and did what I was told to the best of my ability. This parable sums up this whole experience. *"And he said, "The kingdom of God is as if a man should scatter seed on the ground. He sleeps and rises night and day, and the seed sprouts and grows; he knows not how. The earth produces by itself, first the blade, then the ear, then the full grain in the ear. But when the grain is ripe, at once he puts in the sickle, because the harvest has come.""* Mark 4:26-29 ESV.

The key words in this parable to me are *he knows not how*. I had no idea how the Holy Spirit was making the seed grow in the hearts of those around me. But I also didn't need to know. I just needed to be obedient to scatter the seed and trust that the Holy Spirit is going in front of me tilling up the fallow ground of the hearts of people. Sow the Word. It is as simple as that. That is what Regine did to me. She sowed the Word of God and simply loved me despite my sin. That was the model I followed. It was not a man-made model but rather it was a Biblical model. I can only say that the Glory goes to God Almighty. The credit is all His. He is the One who brought salvation to those around me. Amen and Amen. Praise the Lord for He is Good.

FIVE POINTS TO CLEARLY PRESENT THE GOSPEL

We Are Sinners
When Adam and Eve sinned, they were separated from God because God cannot be in the presence of sin. Isaiah 59:2 *"but your iniquities have made a separation between you and your God, and your sins have hidden his face from you so that he does not hear."* Isaiah 59:2 ESV.

We Need a Savior
And because we are separated from God because of our sin, we need a Savior because we cannot save ourselves. We are considered dead in our sin and therefore can do nothing to save ourselves for we have all sinned and that leads to death. *"for all have sinned and fall short of the glory of God,"* Romans 3:23 ESV. *"For the wages of sin is death, but the free gift of God is eternal life in Christ Jesus our Lord."* Romans 6:23 ESV.

Jesus Is The Remedy
The only remedy to bridge the separation between us and God our Creator was to to send Jesus to be the perfect sacrifice for all of mankind. ""*For God so loved the world, that he gave his only Son,*

that whoever believes in him should not perish but have eternal life." John 3:16 ESV.

He Died for Our Sin

Christ Jesus was the only sacrifice for the forgiveness of sins. He died to take away our sin once and for all. And because of this He is the only way to the Father *"but God shows his love for us in that while we were still sinners, Christ died for us."*
Romans 5:8 ESV. *"And by that will we have been sanctified through the offering of the body of Jesus Christ once for all."* Hebrews 10:10 ESV.

Repent, Believe and Confess Jesus

"But to all who did receive him, who believed in his name, he gave the right to become children of God," John 1:12 ESV. *"because, if you confess with your mouth that Jesus is Lord and believe in your heart that God raised him from the dead, you will be saved."* Romans 10:9 ESV.

SCRIPTURES TO MEMORIZE AND PRAY

As we are walking in the Spirit of God, we need to make sure we pray without ceasing. As I have explained how to pray Colossians 4:2-6 over our lives, I want to suggest that we memorize prayers that are in the Scriptures. The Apostle Paul has several that he prayed which are awesome for us to memorize. There are some in the Psalms that are awesome as well.

Here are some of the Scriptures I often use:

"And so, from the day we heard, we have not ceased to pray for you, asking that you may be filled with the knowledge of his will in all spiritual wisdom and understanding, so as to walk in a manner worthy of the Lord, fully pleasing to him: bearing fruit in every good work and increasing in the knowledge of God; being strengthened with all power, according to his glorious might, for all endurance and patience with joy; giving thanks to the Father, who has qualified you to share in the inheritance of the saints in light. He has delivered us from the domain of darkness and transferred us to the kingdom of his beloved Son, in whom we have redemption, the forgiveness of sins." Colossians 1:9-14 ESV.

"I do not cease to give thanks for you, remembering you in my prayers, that the God of our Lord Jesus Christ, the Father of glory, may give you the Spirit of wisdom and of revelation in the knowledge of him, having the eyes of your hearts enlightened, that you may know what is the hope to which he has called you, what are the riches of his glorious inheritance in the saints, and what is the immeasurable greatness of his power toward us who believe,

according to the working of his great might that he worked in Christ when he raised him from the dead and seated him at his right hand in the heavenly places, far above all rule and authority and power and dominion, and above every name that is named, not only in this age but also in the one to come. And he put all things under his feet and gave him as head over all things to the church, which is his body, the fullness of him who fills all in all." Ephesians 1:16-23 ESV.

"For this reason I bow my knees before the Father, from whom every family in heaven and on earth is named, that according to the riches of his glory he may grant you to be strengthened with power through his Spirit in your inner being, so that Christ may dwell in your hearts through faith—that you, being rooted and grounded in love, may have strength to comprehend with all the saints what is the breadth and length and height and depth, and to know the love of Christ that surpasses knowledge, that you may be filled with all the fullness of God. Now to him who is able to do far more abundantly than all that we ask or think, according to the power at work within us, to him be glory in the church and in Christ Jesus throughout all generations, forever and ever. Amen." Ephesians 3:14-21 ESV.

"And it is my prayer that your love may abound more and more, with knowledge and all discernment, so that you may approve what is excellent, and so be pure and blameless for the day of Christ, filled with the fruit of righteousness that comes through Jesus Christ, to the glory and praise of God." Philippians 1:9-11 ESV.

"Let the words of my mouth and the meditation of my heart be acceptable in your sight, O Lord, my rock and my redeemer." Psalm 19:14 ESV.

"He who dwells in the shelter of the Most High will abide in the shadow of the Almighty. I will say to the Lord, "My refuge and my fortress, my God, in whom I trust."" Psalm 91:1-2 ESV.

"Have mercy on me, O God, according to your steadfast love; according to your abundant mercy blot out my transgressions. Wash me thoroughly from my iniquity, and cleanse me from my sin! For I know my transgressions, and my sin is ever before me. Against you, you only, have I sinned and done what is evil in your sight, so that you may be justified in your words and blameless in your judgment.

Behold, I was brought forth in iniquity, and in sin did my mother conceive me. Behold, you delight in truth in the inward being, and you teach me wisdom in the secret heart. Purge me with hyssop, and I shall be clean; wash me, and I shall be whiter than snow. Let me hear joy and gladness; let the bones that you have broken rejoice. Hide your face from my sins, and blot out all my iniquities. Create in me a clean heart, O God, and renew a right spirit within me. Cast me not away from your presence, and take not your Holy Spirit from me. Restore to me the joy of your salvation, and uphold me with a willing spirit. Then I will teach transgressors your ways, and sinners will return to you." Psalm 51:1-13 ESV.

THREE WAYS TO PRAY

The Bible makes it clear that we are to have Scripture in front of our eyes at all times. When proclaiming Christ Jesus, we need to have Scriptures memorized so we can present Christ to the lost. We need not give them chapter and verse but rather because we have memorized them, we can paraphrase and explain the Scriptures clearly within conversations. *"Let your speech always be gracious, seasoned with salt, so that you may know how you ought to answer each person."* Colossians 4:6 ESV.

There are three areas to pray for when proclaiming Christ Jesus. Pray for the lost, pray for yourself, and pray for effectiveness. As we pray in these areas, here are some guidelines to consider. Remember as we sow the seed to the Gospel, we want it to ultimately be sown into fertile ground.

Pray for the Lost

Pray the lost have their hearts tilled up *"Sow for yourselves righteousness; reap steadfast love; break up your fallow ground, for it is the time to seek the Lord, that he may come and rain righteousness upon you."* Hosea 10:12 ESV.
Pray the lost have the veil lifted *"But their minds were hardened. For to this day, when they read the old covenant, that same veil remains unlifted, because only through Christ is it taken away."* 2 Corinthians 3:14 ESV.
Pray the lost see their need for a Savior *"for all have sinned and fall short of the glory of God,"* Romans 3:23 ESV.
Pray the lost hear the Word of God *"How then will they call on him in whom they have not believed? And how are they to believe in him*

of whom they have never heard? And how are they to hear without someone preaching?" Romans 10:14 ESV.

Pray the lost understand and have faith for salvation *"So faith comes from hearing, and hearing through the word of Christ."* Romans 10:17 ESV.

Pray For Yourself

Pray for yourself that there would be opportunity *"At the same time, pray also for us, that God may open to us a door for the word, to declare the mystery of Christ, on account of which I am in prison —"* Colossians 4:3 ESV.

Pray that you would have the Words to speak *"and also for me, that words may be given to me in opening my mouth boldly to proclaim the mystery of the gospel,"* Ephesians 6:19 ESV.

Pray that you would have boldness *"and also for me, that words may be given to me in opening my mouth boldly to proclaim the mystery of the gospel,"* Ephesians 6:19 ESV.

Pray that you would have discernment *"And it is my prayer that your love may abound more and more, with knowledge and all discernment, so that you may approve what is excellent, and so be pure and blameless for the day of Christ, filled with the fruit of righteousness that comes through Jesus Christ, to the glory and praise of God."* Philippians 1:9-11 ESV.

Pray For Effectiveness

Pray that the Word of God would be clear *"that I may make it clear, which is how I ought to speak.* Colossians 4:4 ESV.

Pray that the seed sown will take root *"As for what was sown on good soil, this is the one who hears the word and understands it. He indeed bears fruit and yields, in one case a hundredfold, in another* *sixty, and in another thirty.""* Matthew 13:23 ESV.

"so that Christ may dwell in your hearts through faith—that you, being rooted and grounded in love," Ephesians 3:17 ESV.

Pray that God makes it grow *"I planted, Apollos watered, but God gave the growth. So neither he who plants nor he who waters is anything, but only God who gives the growth. He who plants and he who waters are one, and each will receive his wages according to his labor. For we are God's fellow workers. You are God's field, God's building."* 1 Corinthians 3:6-9 ESV.

Made in the USA
Columbia, SC
25 June 2024